# THINGS NEAR AND FAR

Copyright © 2017 Read Books Ltd.
This book is copyright and may not be
reproduced or copied in any way without
the express permission of the publisher in writing

**British Library Cataloguing-in-Publication Data**
A catalogue record for this book is available from the
British Library

# Arthur Machen

Arthur Machen was born in Caerleon, Monmouthshire, Wales in 1863. At the age of eleven, he boarded at Hereford Cathedral School, where he received a comprehensive classical education. Family poverty ruled out going to university, and Machen was sent to London, where he sat entrance exams at medical school but failed to get in. In the capital, he lived in relative poverty, working in a variety of short-lived jobs and exploring the city during the evenings. However, he began to show literary promise; in 1881, at the age of just eighteen, he published a long poem, 'Eleusinia', and in 1884, he published his second work, the pastiche *The Anatomy of Tobacco*.

By 1890, Machen was publishing in literary magazines, and writing stories with Gothic and fantastic themes. His first major success came in 1894, with the novella *The Great God Pan*. Although widely denounced by the press as degenerate and horrific because of its decadent style and sexual content, it has since garnered a reputation as a classic of horror; indeed, author Stephen King has called it "maybe the best [horror story] in the English language." Machen next produced *The Three Impostors* (1895), a novel composed of a number of interwoven tales which are now regarded as some of his best works.

Between 1900 and 1910, Machen dabbled in acting,

and published what is generally seen as his *magnum opus*, *The Hill of Dreams* (1907). He accepted a full-time journalist's job at Alfred Harmsworth's *Evening News* in 1910, where he remained throughout the war, not leaving until 1921. Machen accepted this role mainly to pay his bills – fiction-writing was his true passion, and he carried on producing novels and short stories throughout the 1910s – but he came to be regarded as a great Fleet Street character by his contemporaries.

The early 1920s saw something of a Machen boom; his works became popular in America, and he brought out his two-volume autobiography. However, by 1929 he was struggling financially again, and left London with his family. It was only a literary appeal launched on the occasion of his eightieth birthday – which drew contributions from admirers such as T. S. Eliot and Bernard Shaw – that eventually ended Machen's money woes. He died some years later in Beaconsfield, Buckinghamshire, England, aged 84. His legacy remains formidable; his work has influenced countless other artists, and is seen as setting the stage for – amongst other things – the Cthulhu horrors of H. P. Lovecraft.

# Things Near and Far

*by*

Arthur Machen

## Chapter I

THE road from Newport to Caerleon-on-Usk winds, as it comes near to the old Roman, fabulous city, with the winding of the tawny river which I have always supposed must be somewhat of the colour of the Tiber. This road was made early in the nineteenth century when stage-coaching came to perfection, for the old road between the two towns passed over the Roman bridge—blown down the river by a great storm in the seventeen-nineties—and climbed the break-neck hill to Christchurch. Well, this new road as I remember it was terraced, as it were, high above the Usk to the west, and above it to the east rose a vast wood, or what seemed a vast wood in 1870, called St. Julian's Wood, of some fame as a ghostly place. It was cut down long ago by an owner who thought timber of high growth better than ghosts.

On the one side, then, the steep dark ascent of St. Julian's Wood; on the other, the swift fall of the bank to the yellow river, where, likely enough, there would be a man in a coracle fishing for salmon. And then there came a certain turn, where suddenly one saw the long, great wall of the mountain in the west, and the high dome of Twyn Barlwm, a prehistoric tumulus; and down below, an island in the green meadows by the river, the little white Caerleon, shining in the sun. There is a grey wall on one side of it, a very old and mouldering wall to look at, and indeed it is old enough, for it is all that remains of the Roman wall of Isca Silurum, headquarters of the Second Augustan Legion.

But there, white in the sun of some summer afternoon of fifty years ago or so, Caerleon still stands for me shining, beautiful, a little white city in a dream, with the white road coming down the hill from Newport, down out of St. Julian's Wood, and so to the level river meadows, and so winding in a curve and coming to the town over the bridge.

That is my vision of the place where I was born; no doubt the recollection of driving home beside my father on some shining summer afternoon of long ago; but of later years another vision of the same white town and white road has come to me. I have "made this up," as the children say, though, no doubt, it is all true. The time now goes back from the early 'seventies to the early 'fifties, and two young ladies are setting out from the Vicarage—it stood practically in the churchyard, pretty well in the position of that other, that illustrious Vicarage at Haworth, and my Aunt Maria could never see any reason why a vicarage should not be in a churchyard—the two young ladies closed the Vicarage door, and made their way down the deserted street, where the grass was green between the cobble-stones, and so passed over the bridge and into the Newport road. They were going to meet John, home from Jesus College, Oxford; and no doubt they talked eagerly of how well John was doing at Oxford, and wondered when he would be ordained, and where his first curacy would be, and what a good clergyman he would make, and how they hoped he would marry somebody nice, and what a pity it was that John was not at home when Mr. Tennyson came to Caerleon and stayed at the Hanbury Arms, and smoked a black clay tobacco pipe with his feet on the mantelpiece; very odd, but poets always were odd people and " Airy Fairy Lilian " was very pretty. The Vicar had called of course, and had been a little shocked at the pipe; still, Papa was always so amiable and ready to make allowances.

" Your grandfather," Aunt Maria said to me years afterwards, " was a most amiable man, but he could not bear radishes or the *Adeste fideles.*"

Well, the two young ladies, Anne and Maria, shading themselves from the heat of the sun with their fringed parasols, pace decorously along the Newport road discussing these and many other matters; parish-matters, of helping poor people and old people and sick people; county matters, the great doings that there would be at the Park when Sir (?) Hanbury Leigh was to have a great party from London on August 12th to shoot grouse on the mountain; Church matters; how a Mr. Leonard had just been given the living of Kemeys Commander and had actually been heard to say, " I call myself a Catholic priest " and, in spite of the Creeds, wasn't that going rather far? And what would John say to that? And, somehow, I fancy the talk came circling again and again back to John, and how glad he would be to be at home again, and how lucky it was that Mrs. Williams Pantyreos had come in that very morning because John always said that he never got butter like the Pantyreos butter anywhere, and how it was to be hoped that the weather would keep up till Wednesday when they were all going to drive to Aunt Mary's at Abergavenny—except Mamma, who said, " Young gadabout ne'er won a clout "—and how this beautiful sunshine must be doing Cousin Blanche's cough a great deal of good : John would like to see Cousin Blanche again.

And so on, and so on, and the two sisters walk along the white limestone road, picking a flower now and again, for Anne paints flowers and Maria is much interested in Botany—I am not sure whether she had acquired Miss Pratt's three-volume work on the subject at that date. And the evening draws along, and the sun hangs over the huge round of Mynydd Maen in the west, and the scents of St. Julian's dark, deep wood fill the stilled air ; till Maria says suddenly : " Anne ! here is the omnibus at last, and, there ! I believe I can see John's face."

The old dim yellow and faded chocolate omnibus from the Bull—I remember it in its last days just before they made the line, and never will I speak of *this* omnibus as a 'bus—comes lumbering on its way, and the old driver, recognising the " two Miss Joneses the Vicarage " and knowing that Master John is inside, causes it to stop. John, a mild-looking young man with little side whiskers, gets

## Things Near and Far

out and kisses his sisters; and the three then get in, and the omnibus lumbers down the hill towards Caerleon, the three chattering of Oxford, of plans and prospects, of Caerleon news and how happy Papa looked at breakfast. And so the evening draws on and the shadows deepen and the walls of white Caerleon glimmer and grow phantasmal like the old grey Roman wall as they cross the bridge and the Usk swims to high tide, the tawny yellow tinged with something of the sunset redness that glows over the mountain. The three are talking and chattering all the while, making plans for holidays and happiness and long bright years and the joy of life—a correct joy, but still joy—before them, and John is enquiring eagerly after Cousin Blanche and nodding and smiling to the Bluecoat boys and girls and saying: "I'll unpack my box to-night and show you my prizes—Parker's 'Gothic Architecture,' in three volumes, and Hooker and a lot more," and they are hoping again and again that Wednesday will be fine, and Blanche is sure to be quite well by this, and John is feeling his young cheeks grow a little red when—it is night.

Alas! They are all dead, years and years ago. The kind Vicar and his grim, good wife are dead. Poor Cousin Blanche perished of consumption in her fresh youth; no summer sun could allay the racking of that cough of hers. Anne followed her, by the same way to the same end: I have the "Holy Dying" that John, my father, gave her. There are two inscriptions in it; one facing the rubricated title-page, now "foxed" with time. This runs:

*Things Near and Far*

> To Anne E. Jones
> from her affectionate
> Brother John Edward
> On her Birthday, and in
> remembrance of the 29th
> September, 1857*
> April 16th, 1858.

The other, on the recto of the leaf, is as follows:

> Johannes Edvardus Jones,
> In memoriam A.E.J.J.
> Quæ obdormvit in Jesu
> 29 mo Martii MDCCCLIX

And those of the party that lived longer knew more of sorrow, and more of broken hopes and of dreams that never came true. And thus, advisedly, I begin this second chapter in the story of a young man's dreams and hopes and adventures. *Ego quoque*—I am forgetting my Latin tags—I, too, have walked on the white road to Caerleon.

To walk a little faster, to comply, in fact, with the request of the whiting in Lewis Carrol's beautiful Idyll, the end of 1884 and the beginning of 1885 found me in something of a backwater. "The Anatomy of Tobacco," the book I had written in the 10 by 6 cell in Clarendon Road, Notting Hill Gate, had been published in the autumn of 1884, and soon after I had set about the translating of the "Heptameron." Every evening I worked at this task till it was ended; and now it

---

\* The date, I think, of their father's death.

was done, and there seemed nothing to do next. I wandered up and down the country about Llanddewi Rectory in my old way, lost myself in networks of deep lanes, coming out of them to view woods that were strange and the prospect of hills that guarded undiscovered lands. Thus on my wider and more prolonged travels, but I had haunts near home, nooks and retreats where nobody ever came. There was an unfrequented lane, very dark, very deep, that led from a hamlet called Common Cefn Llwyn— the Ridge of the Grove—to Llanfrechfa, used scarcely at all save by labouring men going to their work in the early morning and returning in the evening. All the length of this lane there was only one house in sight—the farms in Gwent are mostly in the heart of the fields, remote even from the byways—and this one house must have fallen into ruin eighty or a hundred years ago. From what remained one judged that it had been the *petit manoir* of some dead and forgotten race of little squires; it was of grey stone, of fifteenth-century workmanship, and the corbels supporting the chimney were still sound and clean cut. All about the old broken house were the ruins of the garden, apple trees and plum trees run wild, hedges that had become brakes, a confusion of degenerate flowers; and by the tumbledown stile that led to this deserted place I would linger for an hour or more, wondering and dreaming and setting my heart on the hopeless endeavour of letters. Weather made no difference to my goings; a heavy greatcoat, boots with soles an inch thick, and leather gaiters up to the knee, made a wild wet winter's day a thing to be defied and enjoyed; and indeed I loved to get abroad on such days and see all the wells of the hills overflowing and rushing down to swell the Soar or the Canthwr, red and foaming, and making whirlpools of barmy froth as they fell into the brooks. And then, when the rain changed to snow, what a delight to stand on some high, lonely place and look out on the wide, white land, and on the hills where the dark pines stood in a ring about some ancient farm: to see the wonder of the icy sunlight, of the violet winter sky. These were my great adventures, and I know not whether in reality there are any greater, since it is a great thing to stand on the very verges of an unknown world.

So the winter of '84–85 went on and I dreamed and wondered and did nothing, though I was nearing the age at which many a young man has produced his first novel with success and acclaim. I never could do these things, and still I cannot do them. I knew that I had no business to be loafing and mooning about the rectory, a burden on my poor father—the "John" of that happy return of the 'fifties had by this time experienced sorrows and pains and miseries of all sorts. My mother had been a hopeless invalid for fifteen years, my father's health had failed and he had become very deaf, the poor "living" of Llanddewi Fach had grown poorer still through the agricultural smash of 1880, he was in dire and perpetual straits for money, he underwent most of the mortifications which are allotted to the poor. It makes me grieve to this day to remember with what piteous sadness he would lean his head on his hand ; he had lost hope ; nothing had any savour for him any more. And seeing this, I was distressed to be an additional weight in the heavy pack of sorrows and trials that he bore daily, and I tried to get all sorts of employments for which I was utterly unfit, which would not have harboured me for twenty-four hours. Nothing came of these attempts, and so the time went on till we were in June, 1885. Then there was a letter from the publisher of " The Anatomy of Tobacco " to the effect that he thought he could find me some odd jobs of work if I would come up to London ; and so I returned again to the well-remembered cell in Clarendon Road.

With mixed feelings. I was glad indeed at the prospect of doing something for myself and so removing a little from the weary burden at the rectory : but, I had not forgotten the *peine forte et dure ;* the dry bread, enough and no more than enough, the water from a bitter runnel of a sorrowful street, the heavy weight of perpetual loneliness. " Alone in London " has become a phrase, it is a title associated, I think, with some flaring melodrama ; but the reality is a deadly thing. I was only twenty-two ; and I shuddered a little one June night when I went out and bade farewell to the brooks and the woods and the flowers ; to the scent of the evening air.

All sorts of odd jobs and queer jobs awaited me. I was given a big folio book full of cuttings on a particular subject, and the publisher asked me to make a selection from these and so compile a book of oddments. Then, there were novels submitted to him that I was to read and advise upon : a weary business when the said novels were as a rule foolish things written in varieties of straggly and scraggy scripts. But the principal business was the making of the Catalogue. For the publisher of York Street was also a second-hand bookseller. He had a mass of odd literature stored in a garret in Catherine Street, and on these volumes I was let loose; my main business being to write notes under the titles, notes describing the content of the books and setting that content in an alluring manner before the collector.

It was as odd a library as any man could desire to see. Occultism in one sense or another was the subject of most of the books. There were the principal and the more obscure treatises on Alchemy, on Astrology, on Magic; old Latin volumes most of them. Here were books about Witchcraft, Diabolical Possession, " Fascination," or the Evil Eye; here comments on the Kabbala. Ghosts and Apparitions were a large family, Secret Societies of all sorts hung on the skirts of the Rosicrucians and Freemasons, and so found a place in the collection. Then the semi-religious, semi-occult, semi-philosophical sects and schools were represented : we dealt in Gnostics and Mithraists, we harboured the Neoplatonists, we conversed with the Quietists and the Swedenborgians. These were the ancients; and beside them were the modern throng of Diviners and Stargazers and Psychometrists and Animal Magnetists and Mesmerists and Spiritualists and Psychic Researchers. In a word, the collection in the Catherine Street garret represented thoroughly enough that inclination of the human mind which may be a survival from the rites of the black swamp and the cave or—an anticipation of a wisdom and knowledge that are to come, transcending all the science of our day.

Which? It seems to me a vast question, and I am sure it is utterly insoluble. Of course, an enormous mass of occultism, ancient and modern, may be brushed aside at once without the labour of any curious investigation. Madame Blavatsky, for example, her coadjutors and assessors and successors need not detain us. I do not mean that every pronouncement of Theosophy is false or fraudulent. A liar is not to be defined as a man who never by any chance speaks the truth. A thief occasionally comes honestly by what he has. I mean that the specific doctrines and circumstances of Theosophy: the Mahatma stories, the saucers that fell from the ceiling, the vases that were found mysteriously reposing in empty cupboards, the Messiahship of a gentleman whose name I choose to forget: all this is rubbish, not worth a moment's consideration. And so with Spiritualism; though in a less degree. For I am strongly inclined to believe that very odd things do sometimes happen amongst those who "sit," that some queer—and probably undesirable—psychic region is entered; and all this quite beyond and beside the intention or understanding of those present at the séance. You never know what may happen when a small boy pokes his fingers carelessly among the wheels and works of a clock. But as to the profession of the Spiritualists; that they are able to communicate with ghosts, *that* need not trouble us. Their photographs of fairies need not trouble us. Their revelations as to the life of the world to come as given through the Rev. Vale Owen need not trouble us. Though here is a " phenomenon " which seems to me of no little interest. How can a man who is confessedly perfectly honest and straightforward conjure himself into the belief that when he takes up a pencil an intelligence apart from himself guides his hand as he writes ? I suppose the answer involves the doctrine of dual or multiple personality; and *that* is mysterious enough in all conscience. Yet, apart from all the nonsense, apart from the state of mind of the average Spiritualist—one of them, a very eminent one in his day, said that the clause of the Creed : " I look for the Resurrection of the Dead " meant "I expect to see some physical manifestations of the departed "—apart from all this I still think as I have said that very strange and inexplicable things do sometimes happen. Here is nothing to do with ghosts : but the evidence that the famous medium Home rose into the air, floated out of an open window high on a Scottish castle tower and floated in again at another open window : the evidence here is good ; that is, if levitation, as they call it, were a criminal offence and Home had been put on his trial he would have been convicted. It will be seen that I am not exactly a fanatical Spiritualist : but I had rather be of the straightest sect of Rappers and Banjo Wielders than of that company which understands all the whole frame and scheme of the universe so thoroughly and completely that it is absolutely certain that levitation

## Things Near and Far

is impossible, that a man cannot rise into the air unless he is mechanically and materially impelled and supported, that no evidence, however direct and unimpeachable, can establish this for a fact. I do not understand the universe; consequently I do not dare to advance any such proposition. And further; let me diminish a little a proposition that I have only just dared to make. I have said that all the ghost business, all the Vale Owen sort of business, is rubbish and foolery. Well, I believe most heartily and profoundly that it *is* rubbish, nonsense, unveridical to the last degree; in fact, and in the proper sense of the word, a lie. Yet; let us beware. Not one of us understands the universe. Even in the Higher Mathematics, the Queen of profane sciences, very odd things are reported to happen. So, possibly, the following account may really correspond with the truth of things.

The room is in total darkness. One of the sitters proclaims with exultation that his nose has been tweaked by *Joey*, who, on this side, was a clown. *John King*, understood to have been a master-mariner, sings "Tom Bowling" in a falsetto voice through a speaking trumpet. On this, Cardinal Newman, known to be a lover of music, is gratified and utters the word "Benedictine." There is a sudden scream of joy in a female voice: "Oh! darling Katy, thank you, thank you, *thank you!* Oh, *please*, may we have the lights turned up for a moment? Katy promised me a lock of her beautiful golden hair, and I am *sure* I felt it float down on my hand." The lights are turned up. A strand of yellow hair is, sure enough, reposing on the lady's hand. It had evidently been treated with spiritual peroxide, made, no doubt, of Ethers, like the ghostly whiskey and sodas in " Raymond." Then the room is darkened and the Medium takes up the tale.

" This spirit's name is Milton. Henry—no, John Milton, the author of the ' Faery Queen.' He says that he is very happy. He spends most of his time with Shakespeare and Ben Jonson. Shakespeare has confessed to him that all his plays were written by Bacon. The evidence will be found in a brass box under the Tube station at Liverpool Street. Pope often has tea with him. He says they don't use alcohol there."

There is a sudden crash. " Avast ! " comes with a roar through the trumpet. *John King* has returned, bringing with him an *American Indian* who speaks in the idiom of a Nigger Minstrel practising in the East End of London and will call the Medium his " Midi." Whereupon Katy puts a beautiful warm arm round the neck of a gentleman sitter and the gramophone plays " Abide with me." All repeat the Lord's Prayer, and Sir Arthur Conan Doyle expresses his intense gratification.

Well ; it may be so. But I hope it isn't, and I shall never believe that it is so.

Well ; there I laboured in the Catherine Street garret amidst all this, and much more than this. Down below were the publishing offices of old Mr. Vizetelly, who was issuing English translations of Zola at the time, and was at last sent to gaol for publishing an English version of " La Terre," an obscene book that every judicious Bishop of Central France should put in the hands of newly ordained priests—if it is to be accepted that the physician ought to have some knowledge of the constitutions of his patients and of the diseases from which they are suffering. It was a sumptuous and rich garret—a street now passes over the site of the house—filled with that mysterious odour that used to prevail in oldish London houses that were not too carefully swept and washed and polished, and there day after day I worked, reading and annotating, and all alone. Now and then in the older books I came across striking sentences. There was Oswaldus Crollius, for example—I suppose his real name was Osvald Kroll—who is quoted by one of the characters in " The Great God Pan." " In every grain of wheat," says Oswaldus, " there lies hidden the soul of a Star." A wonderful saying; a declaration, I suppose, that all matter is one, manifested under many forms; and, so far as I can gather, modern science is rapidly coming round to the view of this obscure speculator of the seventeenth century; and, in fact, to the doctrine of the alchemists. But I would advise any curious person who desires to investigate this singular chamber of the human mind to beware of over-thoroughness. Let him dip lightly from the vellum quarto into the leather duodecimo, glancing at a chapter here, a sentence there; but let him avoid all deep and systematic study of Crollius and of Vaughan, the brother of the Silurist, and of all their tribe. For if you go too far you will be disenchanted. Open Robert Fludd, otherwise Robertus de Fluctibus, and find the sentence : *Transmutemini, transmutemini de lapidibus mortuis in lapides philosophicos vivos*—Be ye changed, be ye changed from dead stones into living and life-giving stones. This is a great word indeed, exalted and exultant ; but beware of mastering Fludd's system—if confusion can be called a system—of muddled alchemy, physical science, metaphysics and mysticism. Get Knorr von Rosenroth's " Kabbala Denudata," vellum, in quarto, and find out a little about the Sephiroth : about Kether, the Crown ; Tiphereth, Beauty ; Gedulah, Mercy ; Geburah, Justice or Severity. Really, you will discover very curious things, and the more easily, if instead of Knorr von Rosenroth, you choose A. E. Waite's " Doctrine and Literature of the Kabalah." It is odd, for example, to discover that the side of Mercy is the masculine side, that Justice or Severity is feminine ; and that all will go amiss till these two are united in Benignity. Again, it is interesting from another point of view to discover that three of the Sephiroth are called the Kingdom, the Victory and the Glory. Is there any connection between these and the ancient liturgical response to the Pater Noster : " For Thine is the Kingdom, the Power and the Glory " ? And then that matter of Lilith and Samael and the Shells or Cortices, the husks of spirits from a ruined world that brought about the Fall of Man ; the strange mystery of that place " which is called Zion and Jerusalem "— duly here comparing Böhme on the Recovery of Paradise when innocent man and maid are joined in love—all this is a wonderful and fascinating region of thought. And beautiful indeed is the saying of one of the Fathers of Kabbalism: that when the lost Letters of Tetragrammaton, the Divine Name, are found there shall be mercy on every side. And here, perhaps, but not certainly, light may be thrown on certain obscure matters of Freemasonry. Dip then, and read and wander in the Kabbala; but do not become a Kabbalist. For if you do, you will end by transliterating your name and the names of your friends into Hebrew letters and finding out all sorts of marvellous things, till at last you back Winners—which turn out to be Losers—on purely Kabbalistic principles.

And here, by the way, I may remark that I have long meditated writing an article called "The Aryan Kabbala," keeping the requirements of occult magazines strictly in view. It would make a pretty article. I should begin by a brief note on the Hebrew Kabbala, explaining how the Sephiroth tell in a kind of magic shorthand the whole history and mystery of man and all the worlds from their source to their end. The Tree of Life—as the Sephiroth arranged in a certain scheme are called—is, in fact, I would point out, at once an account of how all things came into being and a map and an analysis of all things as they now are. As an occult friend once said to me by my hearth in Gray's Inn: "The Tree of Life can be applied to that poker." The Tree of Life, then, is a key to the secret generation and being of all souls and all heavens; it will also analyse for you the little flower growing in a cranny of the wall.

Well; this made clear, I would go on to say: "But what if there be a Kabbala and a Tree of Life of the Aryans as well as of the Semites? What if it tells all the hidden secrets of our beginning and our journey and our ending? What if its august symbols are known to all of us, in every-day and common use amongst us, remaining all the while as undiscerned as the most sacred and mystic hieroglyphics? What if the office boy and the grocer handle every day the signs which tell The Secret of Secrets?"

And then, after all due amplifications and ponderous circumnavigations it would all come out. The Aryan Kabbala is, in fact, the Decad; the ten first numbers. They embody an age-old tradition dating from the time when the ancestors of the Greek and the Welshman, the Persian and the Teuton were all one people. They contained the secret mystery religion of this primitive race, they sank by degrees from their first august significance to become instruments of common use and commercial convenience, just as vestments became clothes. The proof is easy enough. Take the first number of the Decad: one in English, ἕν (in the neuter) in Greek, unus in Latin, un (pronounced " een ") in Welsh, ein in German. And then compare another series of words in these languages: wine, οἶνος, vinum, gwin, wein. Then: two, δύο, duo, dau, zwei; and compare with: water, ὕδωρ, udus, wy (and dwr) wasser. I drop the other terms, or Sephiroth, of the Decad—in Mrs. Boffin's presence—and come to the last two numerals: nine, ἐννέα, novem, naw, neun, compared with new, νέος, novus, newydd, neu. Then finally ten, δέκα, decem, deg, zehn: compare with deck (bedeck) δόξα, decor, teg, schön.

## Things Near and Far

The conclusion, I hope, is evident: we (and all things) proceed from Unity, which is wine, decline to Duality (or a weakened, fallen nature), which is water. Then, after passing through many changes, adventures, transformations, transmutations—undescribed for the reason given—we are renovated, made New—" I will make all things new "—in the last number but one of the Decad, and, in the final term, which is Ten, are reunified in Beauty and Glory.

There! It seems to me wonderfully plausible, and I really think I should have written the article and sent it to some suitable quarter. It is all nonsense, of course, but . . . does that matter?

Well, all that business of the Aryan Kabbala is an absurd digression, but it illustrates well enough the frame of mind likely to be induced by the study of a good many of the books in the Catherine Street garret. Take the interlude and add to it the rich odours of the frowsy, neglected room stuffed with confusions of old books and pamphlets, add to it the old, delightful, picturesque London that was undisturbed in those days. Holywell Street and Wych Street were all in their glory in 1885, a glory compounded of sixteenth-century gables, bawdy books and matters congruous therewith, parchment Elzevirs, dark courts and archways, hidden taverns, and ancient slumminess. There were no great, blatant Australia Houses or Colonial Edifices of any kind about the Strand in those times: instead, we had the beauty and the green lawns of Clement's Inn and the solemn square of New Inn, and Clare

Market communicating tortuously with Great Queen Street by the most evil-smelling by-ways that I have ever experienced—and something of jollity in the air that seems to me to have vanished utterly. Take all these elements and things; and you have me as I worked high up in the vanished house in Catherine Street, preparing the Catalogue that was to be called: " The Literature of Occultism and Archæology "—when the gas lamps in the Strand shone with a brighter light than the arc lamps of to-day.

## Chapter II

SUCH was the scene of my life in the summer of the year 1885. By my odd jobs; a little "reading," a little compiling and a good deal of catalogue making, I just managed to live, earning perhaps as much as a pound a week, one week with another. I do not remember exactly the precise terms on which I worked, but I know that I had a good deal of time on my hands. Part of this time I spent in trying to learn shorthand. I can't think why, for at this period of my life I had no newspaper or secretarial employment in view. I am inclined to think that trying to learn shorthand had become a mechanical habit with me. Then, I resumed my old mooning walks out of London, going westward usually or always, sometimes Acton way and sometimes through Brentford—that curious, dirty, and most fascinating place—to Osterley Park, where in those days you could walk and wander anywhere you pleased, so long, I suppose, as you did not glue your nose to the windows of that mansion. And then I fell to writing again.

Now here is a mystery. It is held, and very properly, that people should keep their mouths shut unless they have something to say; similarly that a man has no business to write unless he has something in his heart which, he feels, cries out to be expressed. But here was I not knowing in the least what I wanted to say, but resolved, even at the cost of much pain and misery, to say it; that is, to write it. There are, of course, people who are said to talk for talking's sake; and so, I suppose, I was suffering from the analogous vice of writing for writing's sake, otherwise known as the *cacoethes scribendi*. I fancy a volume of Hazlitt had fallen into my hands; it had strayed, very likely, into the Catherine Street library, and at first I began to try to write essays, more or less in imitation of this inimitable author. I need scarcely say that I made sad work of it; and happily, no scrap of manuscript survives. And then I fell on Rabelais and on Balzac's "Contes Drolatiques," and wondered and admired hugely and studied both deeply in my long night watches under the gas-jet in the little room in Clarendon Road. I would dine sumptuously on half a loaf of dry bread, green tea made as I liked it, without milk or sugar, with plenty of tobacco by way of dessert; and then to my books and to my wonder. It was not a bad life on the whole, sweetened as it was by the enthusiasm for letters; but the loneliness was an oppression and sometimes a horror. Weeks passed without any human converse beyond brief business dialogue; still, since then I have known far worse days. Poverty and loneliness; these are doubtless evils hard to bear; but they are light indeed; nay, they have their dignity, and the gas-jet of Clarendon Road is not altogether without a halo—when I weigh all this and set it in the balances beside the intolerable degradation of the service of Carmelite House. I often thought in those latter

## Things Near and Far

and most hideous days that my case was somewhat that of a man who had been captured by a malignant tribe of anthropoid apes or Yahoos and was by them tormented and unspeakably degraded; and there was this additional shame and horror: that my degradation and misery were witnessed by rational creatures like myself. I remember how in my last year in the employment of " The Evening News," I was out on some idiotic errand which led me up Wellington Street, past York Street, where George Redway, the publisher of " The Anatomy of Tobacco " and of " The Literature of Occultism and Archæology," had his place of business. In a line, pretty well, with York Street I could see that new street which runs over the site of old Vizetelly's office where the famous fusty garret was. The streets—Wellington Street, Bow Street, York Street—are not much changed in the last forty years, and the gap formed by the new street made me see myself a cloudy young man of twenty-two up in the air labouring amongst the dusty ancient books; all this and all the recollections of the days of dry bread, tea, tobacco and the hopeless but not dishonourable endeavour of literature; all this contrasted with the shameful circumstances of my life as a weary old man of fifty-eight, a man who had known struggles and sorrows and losses; all this, I say, overwhelmed me suddenly. It was almost more than I could endure.

But we go too fast. We are still in the days of the cloudy young man, who is clear that fine literature is an infinitely noble thing, but is not clear upon any other subject whatever. I had my queer books in the mornings and my long lonely walks in the afternoons, and my great books in the evening and far into the night. I remember reading Dante in Longfellow's translation, from beginning to end, and though I could not by any manner of means lift up my heart and mind to the mountain-peak of the Paradise, I divined the majesty I could not comprehend. Don Quixote was always with me, and good company and meat and drink and lights and fire always to me; and so I pass along the dim London streets revolving all these mighty works, a ghostly man amidst the hurrying multitude of the living, and go far afield under dim trees in the West, or sit solitary on a bench near the river in Kew Gardens, looking towards Syon; all the while in a lonely but not an unhappy dream.

It came suddenly to me one night. I was lying awake in my bed; and then it came to me that I would write a Great Romance. A Great Romance! I know it is funny; but it is sorry too. I didn't in the least know what the said Great Romance was to be about; save this, that Rabelais was to have something to do with it, and that my own county, beloved Gwent, was to have much more to do with it. That does not sound very definite; but I believe it is more definite than the actual vision which appeared to me, for this was rather a warm and golden and wonderful glow and radiance than any scheme for a book. I know I lay happy and trembling for a long time and fell asleep happy and awoke happy in the morning, and went out forthwith to buy pens and paper. I had both already, but I felt that the occasion was more than a special one and called for very special purchases. So, at the stationer's shop, near the Holland Park end of Clarendon Road, I got ruled quarto paper, and " Viaduct " pens, and two penholders, and I am pleased that I am writing all this with a surviving penholder of those two; a poor old thing chewed to a stump and battered grievously in its metallic parts. So here was paper, here was pens and penholders; and of course the rest was easy.

There was only this little difficulty. The golden and glowing vision of the night, the announcing of the Great Romance, declined to be more specific. It had no hints to give, it seemed, as to plot; it still veiled the subject of this wonderful book in the dimmest, most religious obscurity. The paper and the pens were ready; but how to begin writing the first line? I had not the faintest notion, so I proceeded to write Prologues and Epilogues, with commentaries on the *magnum opus* which was not even begun. Two of these oddities survive, the Dedication to Humphrey, Duke of Gloucester, as the Patron of men of letters; a dreadful quip founded on the old saying about " dining with Duke Humphrey," which meant that you had not had any dinner. This was worked out with all elaboration and with an attempt at the great manner of Bacon in his most magistral mood. It ran in this vein :

> Truly, then, do we poor folk (men of letters) owe what service we are able to pay Your Grace, who in spite of mean dress and poverty (justly

accounted by Mr. Hobbes for shame and dishonour) is pleased to entertain us at that board, where so great a multitude of our brotherhood has feasted before. For your illustrious line hath now for many generations made it a peculiar glory to supply the needs of lettered men; and as we sit at meat it seems (methinks) as if these mighty men of old did sit beside us and taste with us once more the mingled cup we drink. The ingenious author of Don Quixote de la Mancha must, I suppose, have often dined with the Duke of his age, Mr. Peter Corneille and Mr. Otway, Senhor Camoens, Rare Old Ben, Signori Tasso and Ariosto not seldom: while young Mr. Chatterton the poet did not only dine, but break his fast, take his morning draught, and sup with Your Grace's great-grandfather, till at last he died of a mere repletion.

There! Very solemn and portentous fun, indeed; but what is so solemn as a youngster of twenty-two? Canterbury Cathedral and Westminster Abbey seem gay and light and airy by comparison. *I* like it still, to be sure; but then I am prejudiced, and indeed, there is one sentence that still affects me; that phrase about " the mighty men of old " who seem " to sit beside us and taste with us once more the mingled cup we drink." For in that sentence I see something of the spirit which sustained me, the cloudy young man, the dreamy and obscure and inarticulate young man, of those long-ago days, all through the fire and the darkness of poverty and loneliness and weariness and disillusion. Let us still, if you please, ride the high horse and be as magnificent as we can : I saw myself and, to be frank, I still see myself, as the youngest novice in a great and noble monastic house. The novice is by no means a promising member of the congregation, the Abbot and the Prior and the Master of the Novices have the gravest doubts as to his vocation : the other novices are inclined to indulge in remarks of a jocular and contemptuous kind. But the little, obscure and despised candidate for the triple cord sits in his low place at the board and looks at the pictures on the walls : on the faces where torment and exultation shine with twin fires : on Blessed Bernardus a Baculo, who was beaten to death by the Danes in the ninth century, on the Venerable Servant of God, Marcellinus, who was impaled by the Turk, on St. Eugenius de Compostella, who was shut by the Moors in a horrible dungeon of filth for forty years and at last his visage shone and gave light to the tormentors when they came to end him, on Venerable Raymondus Anglus, who was slowly sliced into little pieces in Cathay, on Blessed Gregory Perrot, whom the ministers of the Virgin Queen attended to at Tyburn in 1590 : on all these brilliant successes of the convent does the little novice gaze with admiring wonder. Well he knows that his picture will never hang on the wall ; still, and after all, he is a member of the congregation to which these, the lucky and happy, belonged ; in a faint sort they are his brothers ; they are *commensales, cohæredes, et sodales.*

Very fine, indeed ; but in the meantime I am

scratching with a somewhat hopeless pen under Clarendon Road gaslight, taking difficulties for solution to lonely places such as Perivale, to the unfrequented parts of Hampton Court; or else, by contrast, to the long black High Street of Brentford, with its creeks and backwaters of the river, where grass and flowers grow on the decks of derelict barges. I find no oracles to help me in any of these promising quarters; there are some very sad nights in the little room over the dry bread, tea and tobacco and the helpless pen. Finally, in a kind of despair, I begin something of which the first scene is to be laid in Gwent, which, later, is to have a voyage in it—there is a great voyage in Rabelais to the Oracle of the Holy Bottle. I read the first chapter. It is quite hopeless; and yet I do not give up hope; I resolve to try again.

But all this time, while the Great Romance refused to move, my worldly affairs were moving fast, and decidedly in the way of destruction. I suppose, having finished the Catalogue, I had done all that the publisher wanted of me. At all events, the stream of employment, never auriferous to any great extent, dwindled and dried up. I had a little, a very little money in hand, I could not possibly call on those poor people at home for help; my landlady in Clarendon Road had a hard struggle of it, I fancy, and I would not cadge on her kindness, even though my board and lodging were far from being luxurious. It seemed to me that at the end of the week I must just walk out of 23 Clarendon Road and go on walking towards the West till I couldn't walk any longer. I admit that the plan was vague, as vague as the plot of the Great Romance, but I could think of no other. And in the meantime—I had three or four days before me—I would write the Epilogue for my book: which was not yet begun.

I set about this task with the utmost relish and enjoyment. For once, I knew what to write about; that was my own position; not in a plain and literal manner, but after the fashion of a decorated fantasy. It would never do to say: "Here am I, a stupid lad who is not worth twopence to anybody, who thinks he can write and can hardly get half a dozen words to stagger on the paper; here am I going out to die in a ditch or to live in a ward of the workhouse": that would never have served. I agree with Mr. Sampson Brass in holding that the truth is often highly unpleasant and inconvenient. Hence the Epilogue to the unwritten book, which survives in the written book, "The Chronicle of Clemendy," a work which is neither great nor a romance, but which answers the description admirably in all other respects. And as the Dedication was made to Humphrey Duke of Gloucester, so the Epilogue is concerned with the same nobleman. So here we are:

> A few days ago His Grace did take me aside into his cabinet, and looking kindly upon me (though some call him a stern and awful noble) said: "Why, Master Leolinus, you look but sickly, poor gentleman, poor gentleman, I protest you're but a shadow, do not your Abbrevia-

tures bring you in a goodly revenue?" (Note the elegant reference to my mysterious shorthand.) "Not so, Your Grace," answered I, "to the present time I have abbreviated all in vain, and were it not for the hospitality of your table, I know not how I should win through." "How goes it then with your Silurian Histories?" (The Great Romance.) . . . "With them, may it please Your Grace, it fares excellently well, and this morning I have made an end of writing the First Journey, containing many agreeable histories and choice discourses." "I believe indeed it will be a rare book, fit to read to the monks of Tintern while they dine. But yet I will have you lay it aside a little, since I have a good piece of preferment for you, an office (or I mistake you) altogether to your taste. What say you, Master Scholar, to the Lordship of an Island and no less an Island than Farre Joyaunce in the Western Seas? How stand you thitherwards? Will you take ship presently?" At hearing this, I was, as you may guess, half bewildered with sudden joy, that is apt to bring tears into the eyes of them that have toiled in many a weary struggle with adversity: I could but kneel and kiss His Grace's hand, and say "My Lord."

Of course, the allusions to "First Journeys" and "Silurian Histories" were put in months later, when I had at length found out what my book was about; at the time, October, 1885, I had not written one word of it. So the Epilogue went on its mellifluous way, and thus ended:

## Things Near and Far

But here is my Paumier, with his parchments, to advise with me concerning a grant of Water Baylage to the Abbey of St. Michael, and also concerning the ceremonies observed in the island at Christmastide. He tells me that the voyage will surely be a rough and tempestuous one, but with the captain of the *Salutation* there need be no fear. And so farewell, till the anchor be dropped in the Sure Haven of Farre Joyaunce.

And indeed, as I was writing the last page of the Epilogue, a letter came for me. I had written to Mr. Quaritch, stating my experience in cataloguing, and asking for employment. Mr. Quaritch wrote very civilly stating that he did not want any cataloguers, but people who knew how to sell books. And I wrote on to my final flourish, with all the more relish. " Ceremonies observed in the island at Christmastide," indeed ! Ceremonies observed at Reading Workhouse, more likely !

But the next morning came a letter from Aunt Maria, that Maria who had walked with Anne to meet John on the white Caerleon road. My mother was dying ; and they sent me the money for the fare, that I might come home.

## Chapter III

IT is a debatable point, I suppose, whether life, taking it all round, by and large, as Mr. Bixby said, is a horrible business. On the one hand, most of us are excessively sorry to quit this world, so, clearly, there must be something to be said for it. But, on the other hand, how endless are the devices which we find to give a seasoning to a dish which is, perhaps, rather insipid than nauseous. I have eaten cold mutton with relish—after smothering it in about half a dozen different condiments, sauces, relishes and salads. So look at all the games we play with desperate earnestness, with a vigour and delight and, sometimes, an asceticism which we give to no office routine or serious employment of our lives. Perhaps we may try and define what "life" means a little later; but, under all ordinary and respectable conventions, I presume that the business of which I have been dimly aware on this day of writing can in no wise be classed as one of the serious employments of life; as, in any sense, a vital part of life according to accepted doctrine, religious, scientific or philorophical. The business of which, I say, I have been dimly aware; for all I have seen of it has been Grove Road, Grove End Road, and Circus Road and all the roads adjacent lined on both sides with motor cars of all sizes, splendours and miseries; the

## Things Near and Far

affair being the last day of the Oxford and Cambridge Cricket Match. And, looking at all this fairly, it comes to this : here are two wickets placed at a certain specified distance from one another on a stretch of turf, and here are men with bats and here are men with balls. Will the men with balls succeed in hitting the wickets, or will the men with bats succeed in hitting those balls away to remote parts of the turf ? And on the whole : are the eleven young men of Oxford or the eleven young men of Cambridge the smarter and more skilled at these pursuits and in the subsidiary pursuit called "fielding," or the art of stopping the ball which the man has hit with the bat from going to a remote part of the stretch of turf ? That, in the very rough, is cricket ; and I want to ask the clergy (if they have any time to spare from their self appointed tasks of meddling in politics, "disapproving" of bookstall novels, and serving tables) what they honestly think Saint Paul would have said, if he had seen twenty-two of his most promising young converts engaged in this cricket business, applauded by a vast multitude of the saints ? I desire to put this question not with a wish to "score"—to use an idiom of the game which we are discussing—but with an honest longing for information. That is : will theologians maintain that the 'Varsity Match and First Class County Cricket generally is a part of serious life, or a serious part of life ? Or, will the scientific people or the philosophical people declare that this game, played as it is played at Lord's with desperate earnestness, is a necessary part of the bodily and mental well-being of the human race? I say the game as played at Lord's, that is the great game; for the case of the old-fashioned, village cricket on the green was somewhat different. Then you had a number of people with two or three hours of leisure before them who found a good deal of fun and relaxation and amusement in bowling balls and hitting balls and running after balls, with intervals of supping of ale, sitting on the bench under the shady tree in front of the village inn; this is a very different matter from the high cricket of our times, just as diverting yourself with a ball, a racket and a net is remote from Mdlle. Lenglen's game at lawn tennis.

And these are the comparatively mild forms of sport. What of rowing till you are blue in the face, what of climbing frightful mountain-peaks, with half an inch of rock between you and a fall of a thousand feet? Why do people do all these things, voluntarily, gladly, enthusiastically? I can only suppose that they do these things to make life tolerable, even entertaining, just as I add tomato sauce, Worcester sauce, pickles, beetroot, cucumber and salad to the cold mutton, to make *that* tolerable and even appetising. It would seem indeed that life must be an awful business, if you have to plaster yourself on the walls of a sheer Alp before you can endure it. This is " drowning " your cold mutton in strong sauce with a vengeance.

And all this by way of a tentative explanation of why I ever wrote anything at all, and still more why I have gone on writing, with brief remissions, ever since the autumn of 1880. This problem, as I have hinted already, is a profound mystery. For, taking

## Things Near and Far

first the plain view of the man in the street, and applying his plain and simple test, I have just been running through a list of my books from 1881 to 1922, and reckoning—it was an easy task—how much money I have made by them. The list contains eighteen titles. Of these, the "Heptameron," "Fantastic Tales," "Casanova" represent more or less laborious translations—"Casanova" runs to twelve sizeable volumes. And my total receipts for these eighteen volumes, for these forty-two years of toil, amount to the sum of six hundred and thirty-five pounds. That is, I have been paid at the rate of fifteen pounds and a few shillings per annum. It seems clear, then, that my literary activities cannot be adequately accounted for on the hypothesis of mere greed and money-grubbing.

And, then, taking another side of the question: consider the debit of toil and endeavour and mortification and disappointment that these forty-two years of book-writing have cost me. I believe that business men, engaged in manufacture, always "write off" a considerable sum for legitimate wear and tear and depreciation of plant. What about the wear and tear of mind and heart and that T,e,a,r, which is pronounced in another manner; what about the depreciation of the plant—a highly important one—of self-confidence that my writing has inflicted on me? I have described some of the pains I endured when I set out to write the thing which afterwards became the "Chronicle of Clemendy," and that was only the beginning of months of hard and agonizing labour. And then I remember another occasion. The "idea" which turned into " The Great God Pan " came to me; again that delicious glow of delight. Now at last I had got hold of a real notion; I had a curious tale, a rare fantasy set in a rarer atmosphere to work upon : I thrilled at my heart as the explorer must thrill as he comes suddenly to the verge of the dark forest, or to the summit of the high mountain and sees before him a new and wonderful and undiscovered land. Well I remember how all this exquisite bliss was bestowed on me, one dark and foggy afternoon of 1890–91, in rooms in Guilford Street, not far from " The Foundling." The foul air shone bright, the dingy street, the dingy room were irradiated : here was happiness almost too keen to be endured. With no delay I got notebook and pencil and proceeded to " lay out " the story; that is, to set down the various scenes and incidents by which the plot was to be developed. Afterwards; the writing, and on the whole I was not altogether so ill-contented—though I daresay that I ought to have been disgusted—till it came to the last chapter. And that simply would not be written. I tried again and again; it was impossible. I could hit on no incident that would convey the required emotion; and at last I put away the uncompleted MS. in despair; I was within an ace of tearing it to bits. But think of the suffering, the misery, the bitter disappointment of those evenings. True it was all a silly thing, a toy; but an authority quoted in " The Water Babies " says that one of the saddest sights in the world is a child crying over a broken toy. My scheme was all silly, I allow; but I had set my heart on it, I had glowed with pride over it : and here it was all broken to pieces in my hands, a sorry, spoilt, piteous thing. True, I found some sort of an ending six months later ; but that was not the same. There was no fun in that. You remember the party in the cabrioily that called on Mrs. Bardell ? There was a dispute about the precise situation of Mrs. Bardell's house, and finally the driver, who had dismounted, led the horse by the bridle to the house with the red door.

Here was a mean and low way of arriving at a friend's house ! No dashing up with all the fire and fury of the animal ; no jumping down of the driver ; no loud knocking at the door ; no opening of the apron with a crash at the very last moment. . . . The whole edge of the thing had been taken off ; it was flatter than walking.

So with me and my story : I got to the house with the red door eventually ; but the whole edge of the thing had been taken off. And so it has been with most of my books ; I get, somehow or other, to the house with the red door, or to a house which I try to persuade myself is just as good ; but on the way in the cabrioily I have suffered so many disappointments that I am in no condition to enjoy the pleasure of Mrs. Bardell's society. I remember that, in writing " The Hill of Dreams," I sat down every night for three weeks with blank paper before me, trying to get the second chapter. On some nights I wrote half a dozen lines, on other nights a couple of pages—before the evening's work went, hopeless, into the drawer. A few months later, having fallen on the wrong path, I had the pleasure of casting aside about 30,000 words that I had written; and by the time the book was at last ended there were two neat piles of MS. in my drawer; the one a little higher than the other. The bigger pile consisted of the folios that I had written and had been forced to reject. And think of what that means: a heartbreak to every other page and the comment of the author on himself and to himself: " You fool! Why do you pass your life in rending your heart, in trying to do the thing that you can't do? Why weren't you brought up to sit by a brazier in the streets, to see that nobody steals the planks and railings and the wood pavement: to do something that with an effort you might be able to do?" Or, to return to our former metaphor: "Don't you see that you haven't the knack of the toy maker? Then why will you persist in trying to make toys which always break in your hands, while you fill the air with lamentable boohoos?"

And yet, as I have said, such has been my employment, with intermissions, from 1880 to 1922. It was like that in 1885–86. Night after night, when my father had knocked out his last pipe at eleven o'clock, did I draw out my papers from the table-drawer and set them under the lamp. Winds came from the mountain of the west and shook the trees about the house and sighed and wailed; snows came from the mountains of the north and whitened the terraced lawn, black clouds drifted over Wentwood, the winter rains scourged the land; and still I wrote on in the silent house;

## Things Near and Far

struggling against the bitter conviction of my incapacity, as a man struggles and claws at the crumbling earth when his foot has slipped and he is over the edge of the cliff. Yet, stubborn, I wrote on late into the night, far into the morning, and as the year advanced I often drew the heavy crimson curtain and looked out after I had put away my papers in the drawer, and saw a red or golden dawn streaming above the forest in the east. And as to the work itself ? Let us not enquire too curiously ; though I have always been proud of my parody of the terms of an ancient writ. *Diem clausit extremum*, he has ended his last day, was the title of the writ, which is moved now and then even in these days : my writ was called *Cyathum hausit extremum :* he has drained his last cup. And then there is the *merum et mixtum cervisium*, and the Charter of *Terra Sabulosa* or Sandy Soil, and the offices of Tankard Marshal and *Clericus Spigotti*, or Clerk of the Spigot ; all choice jests—to adopt the manner of the work in question. But, as I say, let us not enquire too curiously into the merits of " The Chronicle of Clemendy." I am content to abide by the verdict of M. Octave Uzanne, who is held, I believe, to be a good judge of letters. He said that it was " le renouveau de la Renaissance," and that I was sure of my place beside Rabelais and Boccaccio, on the serene, immortal seats. I am surrendering my judgment wholly to that of M. Octave Uzanne.

By the way ; I do not know how it was, but the only copy sent out for review was addressed to " Le Livre," which was then edited by M. Uzanne.

Somehow, no review copies found their way to the English papers. But the MS. had been shown to a pushing young literary gentleman, and he said that if it were properly " cut " it might make a good Christmas book for boys.

And then, again, the question returns : why did I compel myself to undergo all the toil and misery and disappointment that the writing of this " Chronicle of Clemendy " involved ? It was my own choice, nobody stood over me with a stick to force me to do it. Why ? Why do men row themselves into blueness and incipient heart disease at Henley and Putney ? Why do men expose themselves to horrors, miseries and the instant risk of death on all the most desperate mountains of the world ? The answer is the same in all these cases : that cold mutton (or life) is in itself intolerable ; that *Le Gigot de Mouton froid, sauce Cyanide de Potasse* is better than the same dish *nature*.

And, going further, the reason of this odd state of things is plain enough. The fact is, that what we commonly call life is not life at all. All the things that are considered serious, important and vital : the faithful earning of a living, the going to the City every morning to copy letters, keep accounts or float companies ; the toils of the Chancery barrister, of the factory hand, of the doctor, of the shop-keeper, of the mining engineer, the affairs of all the serious and necessary employments of life ; these things are not life at all. They are the curse of life, or, as it is sometimes called, the curse of Adam ; as the theologians might have told us if they had not been too busy over the " curse of alcohol," over the dubious moral influence of " the pictures," over the decidedly frivolous character of the lighter fiction of the day, and the demoralising effects of putting a bob on the winner—this dreadful offence, I believe, is held to " harden the heart " more quickly and thoroughly than any other method. But this curse of getting a livelihood remains profoundly unnatural to man, in spite of his long experience of it : hence his frantic efforts to escape from what he erroneously calls life by running himself red in the face at Lord's, by rowing himself blue in the face at Henley, by drinking methylated spirit, by " putting on " those criminal bobs, by playing mind-torturing games like chess, by knocking small balls into small holes, by climbing Alps—and even by writing books. He will do anything to get away from what are called the serious facts of life and follow any track however desperate, trivial, perilous, or painful, if only those serious facts can be evaded and forgotten, though it be but for a few hours. And so I wrote on, night after night, till the August of 1886 saw my task ended ; and I immediately began to think of what I could write next.

## Chapter IV

I HAVE just been trying to reckon up the various quarters which I have occupied in my forty-two years on-and-off life in London. When I first came up to town in 1880—the year when the play was the thing—I stayed at Wandsworth in an old Georgian house near the ugly Georgian church. I looked for it a few years ago, but I could not find it; I suspect that shops now flourish on its site and on the site of its grave old garden. Then, in 1881–82 I was domiciled in a house fronting Turnham Green; here, too, were ample lawns and gardens which, for all I know, may remain still. Clarendon Road, as I have mentioned once or twice, entertained me in '83, '84, and again in '85, and when I returned to London at the beginning of '87 I lodged for a time in Upper Bedford Place, Russell Square. This place I left for an amusing reason. I had been out rather late. The festivity was not furious; simply a little and most informal dance given by Mrs. Augusta Webster, in those days an admired poetess; and I suppose that it was half-past one when I got home from Hammersmith. I was moving softly up the stairs, and was a good deal puzzled to hear the clanking noise of metal on metal, as I passed the door of the first-floor bedroom. However, I supposed that somebody was ill and that the fire was being kept up.

## Things Near and Far

But the next morning, the landlady addressed me gravely. She said that Mr. and Mrs. Sogden had been very much alarmed by hearing footsteps in the middle of the night, and had made preparations for receiving burglars; and on the whole the landlady thought that I should be much more comfortable at her sister's in Great Russell Street, where no ladies were taken and things "were more Bohemian." And, indeed, she was quite right. The garret—a real garret, with a sloping roof and a dormer window—looked out on Dyott Street, the last remnant of the old rookery of St. Giles; the house was late seventeenth century or quite early eighteenth, and the room, with tea and bread and butter breakfast included, only cost ten-and-six a week. Later in the year, I moved across the street and lived for a while over a stained-glass business; then I crossed again and lived over a tailor's shop. January, 1890, found me in two rooms in Soho Street—undoubted seventeenth century, panelled, with beautifully deep wooden cornices. And here took place the battle of the fleas.

I had moved in, as I say, early in the year, in cold weather. The rooms seemed quite all right, and the black tom cat of the premises was a remarkable and consistent character whom it was a privilege to know. His daily plan of dining with every one in the house, from his own family in the basement to the people in the attics, finally welcoming the cat's-meat man with loud shrieks, shewed, I thought, Mind. And, as I say, the cornice; well, I wish that I had been draughtsman enough to draw a section of it. Well, everything was as pleasant as it could be; and there, at the door, was all Soho to explore and investigate, and I suppose I need not say that Soho offered then, and still offers, I am glad to note, a large and curious field wherein the contemplative mind loves to expatiate.

Very well; but the weather got warmer: and the fleas appeared. At first as single spies; and then in battalions. They swarmed everywhere. They made life hideous and intolerable. I did not see what was to be done. My furniture, such as it was, occupied the rooms; it would be highly inconvenient for me to move. The advertised specifics were useless. I isolated a flea—they were fair, large fleas—with a little of the powder, under a wine glass and watched his behaviour. He seemed happy, though perhaps a little torpid; he reminded me of a stout, red-faced old gentleman who has had two or three glasses of " hot Scotch," and is inclined to fall asleep by the tavern fire. Clearly, such mild measures were useless against the busy multitudes which swarmed all over my rooms. Then, I had a notion, a much more brilliant notion than anything that I have known in the region of literature. I have an odd and random vein of practicality within me, and it came out in the Soho Street emergency. I took a large sheet of newspaper and brushed it over with treacle and laid it on the bedroom floor and waited for an hour or two. At the end of that time, a dozen or so of fleas were sticking fast to the treacle. I experienced the happy glow of the inventor; and now there was no dismal reaction. By the evening, there were at least six dozen fleas captured and out of action. I thought I might say, Eureka.

But then there came a difficulty. I discovered a certain property in treacle, which, so far as I know, is not recorded in scientific text-books. The matter of the work—to use the term of alchemy—was, I found, susceptible to weather. In certain states of the atmosphere, in place of being sticky, it became crystalline and as hard as glass. I do not know whether this interesting property of treacle can be utilised for forecasting purposes. But this hardness rendered it useless for my immediate end. The large, fair fleas hopped on to the trap and hopped away. I surveyed the problem anew. Again the flash akin to genius. I thought of fly-papers and bought half a dozen. The battle was over in a few weeks. I kept a careful daily account, and in a month, or perhaps five weeks, I had captured over three thousand fleas. And I had purged the first floor of 12 Soho Street utterly of all the race. I recollect well one night's bag. I had been to see "A Pair of Spectacles" at the Garrick, and when I came home I found I had got 120 fine fleas.

And then, having won this notable victory, a very odd distaste for London came upon me. I am not joking; the sentiment had nothing to do with the insects whom I had defeated; but, somehow, London sickened me. Its faint, hot summer airs were an oppression, its swarming streets a tribulation; I thought of cold wells in the hills and running brooks and the breath of the wood and the mountain in the early morning—and I resolved to be a countryman again. So I took a cottage high up on the Chiltern Hills, and while certain alterations were being made, I left for Tours, Touraine, France.

The Rabelaisian enthusiasm was still upon me. I had just issued a translation (called "Fantastic Tales") of that extraordinary and enigmatic book, "Le Moyen de Parvenir," by Beroalde de Verville, who was a canon of Tours Cathedral. So to Touraine I went; to see the land of Rabelais, of Beroalde, of Balzac. And the odd thing is, that my first Sunday afternoon in Tours—I got there on a Saturday—was a severe disappointment. The fact was that I had taken Doré's wonderful illustrations to the "Contes Drolatiques" for granted. I supposed that the enchanted heights, the profound and sombre valleys, the airy abysses of these amazing plates represented, with a little exaggeration, perhaps, the veritable scenery of Touraine. You remember the picture showing how that sinful little page climbed the heights of Marmoutiers to confess his sin to the Abbot? Well, that Sunday afternoon, early in September, 1890, I set out from the Faisan, in the Rue Royale, to see the tremendous ascent of Marmoutiers. I crossed the bridge over the Loire, most of it sand with a swift stream here and there, and arrived at Portillon, where the conductor of the steam tram was calling out "Marmoutiers, Rochecorbon, Vouvray" in a melodious chant. But I walked along the road to Marmoutiers. Alas! there were no terrific heights, as in the picture. Imagine something like the high ground near the river at Henley; nothing higher, nothing as high. Instead of the dark green woods

## Things Near and Far

of Henley, golden rocks and golden earth shining in a very happy sun; little villas, larger villas, everywhere with gardens that were gardens indeed. Green walled closes, with rich green lawns; fountains in the midst of them, flowering shrubs and flowery creepers blossoming and trailing everywhere; kitchen gardens where the peaches glowed and burned dark against the hot white walls, where the pears on the dwarf trees were as shapes of golden honey: at last the old *clôture* of the Abbey of Marmoutiers with pepper-pot turrets at intervals, close to the road, and inside the enclosure, the modern buildings of a convent school: and the mellow, river cliff behind all. It was delightful; but it was not a bit like Doré. I confess, my heart sank. And then going on by the river road, I got to Rochecorbon. Still the warm cliff overhung the road, underneath it a small hamlet with a tavern, "A la Lanterne de Rochecorbon," and perched on the edge of the cliff the Lantern, an odd structure which looked something like an ancient factory chimney, and was, I suppose, the sole relic of the ancient castle celebrated by Balzac. It took me some time before I could get Doré's Touraine out of my mind and enjoy the Touraine of actuality on its own merits. And these are many. There were great moments on this first visit to the garden of France.

I was staying at the Faisan in the Rue Royale—that street which Balzac, who was born in it, praises as being "always royal, always imperial," which in these later days has taken to calling itself the Rue Nationale—a delicious inn indeed. I got the recommendation from Thackeray. Philip stayed there once. He calls it the "Faisan d'Or." It had three courtyards, or rather a courtyard and two gardens, both closed in by the hotel walls. You entered the courtyard under the archway in the Rue Royale; to the left was the dining-room hung with tapestries depicting in an ancient mode the famous castles of Touraine; on the right was the kitchen, all bright with glowing copper pots, and the big round cook standing at the open door or bending over his furnace, occasionally shaking one of his pots knowingly and beaming on you as you sat at your little table in the courtyard as much as to say: "You will find it good." Around this great man were four or five boys, all in white like their chief, who seemed to be busy all day long in washing vegetables, in chopping meat and herbs fine for *farses*, in manifold culinary employments, running out now and again and shaking showers from bags full of wet lettuce or endive leaves. At the back were the stables, and on market days the yard of the Faisan was full, like an English inn yard, of all manner of queer traps and shandridans from the country. And beyond this courtyard, at the back of the house, were the two gardens, secret, retired and delicious. Such green turf was there in these chosen places, so pleasant a music in one of them of a singing fountain, so glowing the flowers about it with the water drops glittering on them, so sweet the shade of overhanging boughs—there are here and there gardens that address the heart and spirit and not the florist, as Poe knew well.

And thinking of the Faisan at Tours and of its curious delights, how is it that much money—one may say the wealth of the whole world—cannot buy anything like this in London? Money will get you a set of rooms thirty feet or so in height from floor to ceiling, it will buy you the use of suites of furniture that make you wonder when you wake up in the morning whether by any chance you can have turned into Louis XV in your sleep; it will buy you bathrooms all marble and tessellated pavement, dining-rooms as marblous and Louisquinzious as your private suites; but delights such as are afforded by the Faisan at Tours it will by no means buy. It is a pity; at least I think so. But then I can never fancy that I am Louis XV even for a moment, and that, I suppose, is the reason why I don't like living in the style of that monarch, why I don't even like lunching or dining in palatial halls built and furnished in his favourite manner. And I doubt whether the grandest of all grand hotels in our London could furnish you with a bottle of Vouvray Nature of a named *clos*, for any money that your millionaire's purse could proffer.

And the mention of that admirable amber wine of Vouvray, the wine wherein an argent bead rises at intervals through the mellow gold, reminds me of my first night at the Faisan. All down the tables were portly decanters of wine, red and white. I chose red, and found it a new sensation in wine vastly to my taste. It was, of course, an ordinary wine, and a little wine, I think of the kind called Joué Noble, from the place of its growth, a parish by the Cher river. It was scented like flowers in June; it was in its entirely unpretending way quite exquisite. I drank it with relish, and towards the end of dinner I had accounted for about three-parts of the decanter. Swiftly came the head waiter and bore it away and as swiftly put another and a full decanter in its place. It was almost too much; "temperance" enthusiasts would say a great deal too much. I thought solemnly to myself as I smoked a grateful pipe after dinner in the courtyard: "This night I have had as much good red wine as ever I could drink." And this was one of the great moments of my visit to Touraine.

And then there was Chinon. The train passes through the deep darkness of Chinon Forest, and you leave the station and come out into the sunlight. Here is a narrow river valley: the clear Vienne in the middle of it; to the left a gently rising land, rich with vines; to the right a long, golden, precipitous cliff, golden in such a sunlight as we never see in England. As in the backgrounds of the old Italian masters, the trees stand out clearly, vividly, distinctly against the sky; so was it at Chinon. That long, mouldering and golden cliff was surmounted by the walls of the old castle, golden and mouldering also, irradiated; and from the river to the cliff the town climbed up; narrow ways, winding ways, steep ways, and every here and there the grey-blue *tourelles* of the fifteenth-century houses piercing upwards; and the dark mass of the forest stretching far and far away beyond. And then the thought that the man who had received one of the great visions of reality once walked these ways, and looked on a scene that had not much changed since his time; that the golden and rich sunlight had shone on him also, in the hour when the amazing, terrible, tremendous figures and symbols of the vision of Pantagruel, Panurge, Friar John, the three who are yet one came to him, we must conjecture, in clouds and darkness and uncertainties, as he listened to the new song of the vineyards, and the vine and the outpoured wine: all this was made a great moment also. I sat on a sort of bridge—if I remember—joining the two parts of the ruined castle, sat on golden stones, and looked down on the Chinon of the grey-blue *tourelles*, on the shining Vienne, and the gentle vine-covered slope, and I thought of the cloudy young man stumbling over that hard French of Rabelais far into the night, in obscure Clarendon Road, long ago. It was not long ago; this was of '90 and that was of '85, but hard pains make long years. I went down the hill again, past the fountain, and drank the red wine of Chinon solemnly, reverently in a dark tavern in one of the dark, narrow streets. It was called "Le Caveau de Rabelais."

I came back to London in the autumn and took rooms in Guilford Street till that cottage on the Chilterns should be ready for occupation. Then from 1891 I lived in the country, and found it nothing, and came back to London in the autumn of 1893, to an "upper part" in Great Russell Street, a little westward of the British Museum. It was then that I began to explore London, and to realise its vastness, its immensities. Things are relative; I began now to appreciate the fact that if you set out, without a map, from your house at 36 Great Russell Street and walk for an hour eastward or northward you are in fact in an unknown region, a new world. Continually you stand on a peak in Darien, and look out on undiscovered territories, inhabited by peoples of whom you know nothing. I would go along Great Russell Street, and turn up into Russell Square, and then go by Guilford Street, crossing Gray's Inn Road, and so find myself, like the knight in the song, " ten leagues beyond the wide world's end." I would go northward, up the Gray's Inn Road, and then turn to the right, descend into a valley and climb a height and so come to a region which was to me as the ultimate parts of Libya, and the lands of the Mountains of the Moon. I shall never forget the awe with which I first came upon the other Baker Street, the Baker Street which would enter no taxi-driver's mind; those houses climbing up the hill into Lloyd Square, stucco houses with classic pediments, but all tottering, askew, and falling into decay ; the jerry building of 1820–30. And, I remember, seeing on one of the leaning and doubtful doors here the brass plate of someone who said that he was a " Buhl Maker." I wonder. Did someone really labour in this forsaken, climbing street in that rich eighteenth-century art of brass and tortoiseshell, fashioning curious cabinets and escritoires ! How unlikely it seemed ; more unlikely than another announcement on a modest door in the recesses of Camden Town, to the effect that here were made Shell Boxes.

Often I went up Baker Street and stood in Lloyd's Square and looked down on London, on Gilbert Scott's horrible, villainous sham-Gothic St. Pancras

## Things Near and Far

Station and on all the vague, smoky, weary streets about it. Here, one evening, the sun flamed suddenly and struck the windows of a school below and lit fires in them : hence the lines—in " A Fragment of Life "—entitled : " Lines written on looking down from a Height in London on a Board School suddenly lit up by the sun."

And here I would say that the matter of Wonder—that is the matter of the arts—is everywhere offered to us. It is, I am sure, true, as the feeble though pious Keble wrote, that :

> The daily round, the common task
> Will furnish all we need to ask.

And it is utterly true that he who cannot find wonder, mystery, awe, the sense of a new world and an undiscovered realm in the places by the Gray's Inn Road will never find those secrets elsewhere, not in the heart of Africa, not in the fabled hidden cities of Tibet. " The matter of our work is everywhere present," wrote the old alchemists, and that is the truth. All the wonders lie within a stone's-throw of King's Cross Station.

I remember that when, later on, I wrote a book on the principles of literary criticism called " Hieroglyphics," a good many of the reviewers found grave fault with my dictum that all fine literature is the work of ecstasy and the inspirer of ecstasy. " In other words," said these clever fellows, " a good book is a book that you happen to like. But other people may have very different tastes and likings ; no doubt many people experience ecstasy in reading a newspaper feuilleton. Is the feuilleton therefore fine literature?" The objection, I hasten to say, is perfectly legitimate. Tens of thousands, or hundreds of thousands of people, I have no doubt, read the newspaper feuilleton in an ecstasy of delight. I once found myself, to my dumb, almost awestruck horror, in a drawing-room where a number of tolerably well-educated people were engaged in taking the works of . . . well, Miss Thingumbob, seriously. Doubtless, then, there are many people who find rarities and wonders in matter that you and I pronounce to be contemptible or detestable or just nothing at all : my reviewers were perfectly right. But if you accept their ruling you put an end to criticism of all sorts. I could form a large company of coalheavers, financiers, sporting noblemen, gardeners, journalists, ladies of quality, actors, scavengers—I was going to add bishops, but they rarely speak the honest truth—and myself who had very much rather not see the famous Primavera and the famous Monna Lisa Gioconda than see them, who had rather—again I include myself—listen to George Robey's songs and gags and wheezes than to "Hamlet." But what does that prove? Simply, I suppose, that so far as the pictures and the play are concerned my friends and myself cannot rise to these particular heights. As an old friend of mine once observed very well, "We all of us have some windows that are darkened." My friend is a musician, and remembering his maxim, I was much diverted one day by hearing him speak with easy contempt of the composer of "Acis and Galatea." But it is true that each one of us has some darkened windows : Oscar Wilde confessed

## Things Near and Far

to me once, with shame be it said, that he thought absinthe a detestable drink. But no inference can be drawn from this undoubted fact. It always stirs in me a certain feeling of impatience when I see the solemn correspondence, the more solemn leading articles under the dread heading, " What is Wrong with the Church ? " It is alleged, I am sure with complete truth, that a great many people do not go to church ; and the conclusion is drawn that the Church must be very gravely at fault. Now this may be true also—I think it is—but it is a conclusion not to be deduced from the minor premiss, the sole premiss stated. Scholastic logic, the only logic that is worth twopence, the " new logic " being, as an Oxford graduate once very sensibly observed to me, merely " nonsense about things," is now unfashionable, so, I suppose I shall be thought somewhat boorish for exhibiting the newspaper syllogism at full length, supplying the suppressed major. But here it is :

That which is unpopular is worthless.

The Church is unpopular.

Therefore, the Church is worthless. In other words, as one of the ladies in the cabrioily—to which I have already alluded—observed : " Most Votes carries the day." Very well ; but how does the attendance on the pictures in the National Gallery compare with the attendance at " the pictures " ? And shall we try the experiment of " knocking " the music-halls, the revue houses and the musical comedy houses by running Bach's Organ and Clavier Fugues at popular prices ? Perhaps the purse of Rockefeller might survive the experiment ;

certainly no other purse would hold anything after a year of it. Mr. Walkley of "The Times" proposes to solve the difficulty of criticism by making the critic address himself to ὅ χαριείς, the well-graced and accomplished man. But who is he? Each one of us is a good judge—in his own judgment. And technical instruction is nothing. No one in his senses would seek anything vital as to Greek or Latin poetry from a classical don at Oxford or Cambridge. Keats, poor, shabby John, who had only been to a commercial academy, knew more about Greek poetry than a wilderness of classical tutors.

But, I was going to say, all these considerations apply to the known and recognised arts, to literature, music, painting, architecture. In all these I am willing to admit I may be hopelessly wrong—I have said that I had much rather hear Robey than "Hamlet"—but I will listen to no objections or criticisms as to the Ars Magna of London, of which I claim to be the inventor, the professor and the whole school. Here I am artist and judge at once, and possess the whole matter of the art within myself. For, let it be quite clearly understood, the Great Art of London has nothing to do with any map or guide-book or antiquarian knowledge, admirable as these are; and indeed Peter Cunningham's "London" is to me one of the choicest of books. But the Great Art is a matter of quite another sphere; and as to maps, for example, if known they must be forgotten. How would the Odyssey have read, do you imagine, if Ulysses had been furnished with Admiralty Charts, giving the

## Things Near and Far

soundings in fathoms, even to the exact depth of water in the harbourage of Calypso's isle? And all historical associations; they too must be laid aside. Mr. Pickwick at Bury St. Edmunds has nothing to do with the history of the famous abbey. Of all this the follower of the London Art must purge himself when he sets out on his adventures. For the essence of this art is that it must be an adventure into the unknown, and perhaps it may be found that this, at last, is the matter of all the arts.

And it was this art of London that I followed, while I lived in Great Russell Street between '93 and '95, and still more earnestly afterwards when I was living at Verulam Buildings, Gray's Inn. Sometimes I took a friend with me on my journeys, but not often. The secret of it all was hidden from them, and they were apt to become violent. On one grey day that I remember I had personally conducted a man on a most interesting exploration of the obscurer by-ways of Islington. He grew silent as the streets grew greyer and the squares dimmer and the remoteness of the whole region from any conceivable London that he knew filtered through his soul. His London was Piccadilly, the Haymarket, St. James's, and the many polite neighbourhoods where there are flats and calls are paid and tea is taken and literary and theatrical and artistic circles meet and gather. But this London that was a grey wilderness, these streets that went to the beyond and beyond, these squares which nobody that my friend could ever have known could ever inhabit: it was all too much for him. His face darkened with terror and hate, and with a poisonous glance at me he struck his golden-headed cane violently on the pavement, and stopping dead, exclaimed : " I wish to God I could see a hansom ! "

So, of course, I never took him to Barnsbury. As for Brentford, that is the Great Magisterium, the Hidden Secret. There is a Secret Society of those initiated in Brentford, and so darkly is the mystery kept that there have been cases in which members have known each other intimately for twenty years before the passwords have been exchanged.

## Chapter V

I HAVE been talking of rooms in Gray's Inn, of trips to Touraine; and I suppose it will have become evident that the days of the Clarendon Road cell, of dry bread and green tea meals were over. This was, in fact, the case. Between '87 and '92 I " came into money," that is, into what I called money. My mother died in 1885, my father in 1887; distant and ancient relatives in Scotland who had lived to fabulous ages died at last, and thus moneys that should have come to my mother came to me. And I was no longer the lonely man of the earlier chapters.

Reckoning up the various sums which I inherited, I calculate that if they had been invested I should have had enough whereon to live narrowly and meanly for the next thirty years. Somewhere about 1921 a long lease would have fallen in, and two-thirds of my income would have disappeared. I should then have been left with sixty pounds a year at the outside, and even with the "aconomy" recommended by Captain Costigan, there is very little to be done in these days with £60 per annum. But I did not invest my fortune in sound securities. Perhaps I might have done so if it had fallen in a lump on my lap; but this was not the way of it. It came in bits and parcels: £700 one year, £500 eighteen months afterwards. So I adopted the simple, manly course of putting my money as I got it into a box, as it were, and dipping my hand into the box when I needed a few gold pieces. I wish it were possible to do this literally: it must be magnificent to live on a chestful of gold; but I compromised by getting a cheque-book.

And I have always been glad that I made this business-like arrangement. By it I was enabled to live for eleven or twelve years under pleasant and humane conditions. Not in luxury, be it understood, for luxury has always been utterly detestable to me. Detestable to me, I say with emphasis; I do not say that luxury is detestable in itself. If men like to have it so, by all means let them dwell in marble halls, with vassals and serfs and wine-stewards at their side. Let them be as Louisquinzious as ever they please in their homes and at their hotels; for all I care, they may take their ease in snuggeries, all gold and mirrors and marbles, fifty feet high, a hundred feet high, if they like it so. But to me, a poor clerk, all this has ever been nauseous. When I plied my sorry trade of journalist, I disliked most things involved in that vile business, but I hated my occasional missions to the Hôtel Splendide and the Hôtel Glorieux. I would be sent to these places to find out, say, the exact method employed by the new chef, M. Mirobolant, in cooking red herrings for the famous Joy Teas in the Venetian Hall—everybody has heard of the Joy Teas at the Splendide, and of the Joy Band of twenty kettle-drums, fifty tea-trays, ten trombones and thirty bassoons. Well, I would be sent to the Splendide on this errand; or, perhaps, to the

Glorieux to find out whether it were true that the principals of the Russian Ballet sucked their morning tea through raspberry jam and declared that this was necessary to their art. I would visit one or other of these establishments and sit down on Louis Quinze or Louis Seize chairs and wait there in my dingy old cloak, while " Reception " and " Enquiries " smiled to see such an incongruous figure before them, while the guests of the hotel smiled also as they went in and out, till at last the manager arrived, fretful enough, usually, at being dragged from his business or his leisure to answer idiotic questions. I used to wonder on these Splendide or Glorieux days what I had done to deserve such humiliations. The only thing that somewhat consoled me was the thought that, whatever pains the Doctor may have suffered, while he waited in Lord Chesterfield's outward rooms or was repulsed from that nobleman's door, my case was more humiliating still, since an English nobleman of race is a much greater personage than the shiniest of hotel managers. And perhaps, also, I fancied that I was beginning to follow a little in the faithful steps of Venerable Raymondus Anglus, who was slowly sliced into little pieces in Cathay.

Rather, I am afraid, in the steps of a relative of my own, some distant Cousin Machen, whom business, I suppose, took to Cathay in the 'fifties and 'sixties of the last century. It so fell out that while this gentleman was in China we declared one of our infamous Opium Wars against the Dragon Throne and the Vermilion Pencil. Promptly the local mandarin seized Cousin Machen and put him in a cage. They then travelled him round the Chinese " Smalls." When the cortège got to a village or town, my cousin's custodians touched him up smartly with their spears. Cousin Machen would then dance with anguish, and, I am sure, most ungracefully, and the happy villagers, howling with mirth, and voting Cousin Machen good goods, would pelt the poor man with undesirable matters. He got away from them, but I have heard my relations say that in extreme old age the mere word "China" was enough to bring a sweat of horror pouring down his face. And I am in a position to sympathise fully with Cousin Machen——

Well, I was saying, I think, that I never cared for luxury, and so did not waste my bit of money on it. But if luxury tempts me not at all, I care a great deal for homely comfort, and I lived in considerable comfort in the days of which I am speaking. I think that my annual budget was between four and five hundred a year, and let me tell an amazed generation that for five hundred a year or rather less two people could live very sufficiently in the 'eighties and 'nineties. Your saddle of mutton and your sirloin of beef were of the best, lamb at Easter —is there anything better than spring lamb with its skin roasted to a golden-brown?—was easily attainable; fowls and ducks, grouse and partridges and pheasants, with now and then that most delicious bird the woodcock, were no rarities. And asparagus might well appear quite early in the spring, and green peas in advance of the main crop. And sometimes one felt that it would be amusing to go out to dinner for a change: well, the bill of the Soho restaurant never gave an indigestion afterwards. Sometimes the Soho dinners were quite good, they were always amusing; and in those days there was such a thing as decent Chianti. It came to the cheerful table in flasks of very thin glass, and between the cork and the wine was a stratum of olive oil. This the waiter flicked off on to the linoleum with a swift gesture. The last Chianti of this order that I tasted was in 1902. I saw great gallon flasks of it standing in the window of a small shop opposite the stage door of the Palace, and bought one of these flasks—it cost six shillings, if I remember—and bore it tenderly to my dressing-room at the St. James's Theatre. It was the last night of "Paolo and Francesca," and we drank the Chianti merrily in trunk hose and armour when the play was done. And Herbert Dansey, who was really a noble Florentine, " degli Tassinari," vowed you could get no better Chianti in all Tuscany.

Or again, one didn't fancy roast beef, and yet one didn't want to go out dining. There was the middle course; Salame or Mortadella, half a round of ripe Brie and a bottle of a sufficient red or white wine. And a half-bottle of Benedictine only cost four-and-six. And the whole of the small banquet ran into very little: they were cheap days, and the Income Tax was inconsiderable then. But I was forgetting. I had no income, so I saved the expense of the tax. And under these conditions, living very pleasantly, with a month in France every year, I cultivated literature between 1890–1900. I refrained, utterly, I am glad to say, from the impious folly of wondering what would happen when the money should have come to an end. When that day came, why, that day could see to it.

Living very pleasantly; that is, apart from my chosen sport of making books. I have already discussed the strange paradox of writing, of writing, that is, when it is entirely divorced from all commercial considerations. I wrote purely to please myself; and what a queer pleasure it was! To write, or to try to write, means involving oneself in endless difficulties, contrarieties, torments, despairs, and yet I wrote on, and I suppose for the reason which I have given, the necessity laid upon most of us to create another and a fantastic life in order that the life of actuality may be endurable. Look at the golfer: observe how he toils and frets in that fantastic world that he has made for himself, a world wherein he who can say, "I did the fourth hole in two" is happy; while the wretch who had to hit the little white ball six or seven times before it finally popped into that fourth hole goes out wretchedly into the night. It is fantastic nonsense; but for all that the golfers are in the right.

Still, there may be a little more in the sport of literature; and if the golfers feel hurt by this remark, let them remember that a man always praises his own game. We understand so little of the real scheme of things that, for all we know, golf may be the end for which man was made, as, according to Coleridge, snuff was the final term of the human nose. But waiving this possibility—I think a remote one—I would contend that literature has more in it on the whole. Being an art as well as a sport, there is a question of making something, and very occasionally of making something that will divert or enchant others, besides the maker; whereas the sport which is nothing but a sport has no such by-products as "Don Quixote" or "Pickwick." Of course the man who plays a game, such as golf or cricket, often gives pleasure—or amusement, at all events—to many spectators; but when the match is over and the last ball bowled nothing permanent remains. So far as others are concerned the player of games is much in the position of the player of plays. The actor thrills the house or rocks it with laughter; but the curtain falls and all is over. We know that the best judges of the eighteenth century found Garrick natural, simple, affecting; but we know no more. We have pictures of Garrick in his favourite situations; but I at least have no distinct image in my mind of what it was really like to be in the front row of the pit at Drury Lane and see and hear Garrick play.

And, this apart, I cannot help thinking that the pleasures of the literary game are more intense and more exquisite than the pleasures of the other games. I know this is a very difficult question; there is no final answer to it. But I feel sure that the happiness of Charles Dickens on writing the last words of "David Copperfield" was greater than the happiness of the cricketer at Lord's who carries out his bat for a faultless innings of two hundred against the most difficult bowling and the best fielding in England. I do not know that this is so, but I conjecture that it is so, chiefly because the joys of the writer of a great romance are so varied and so complex in comparison with the joys of the man who has played a perfect innings. In a sense, perhaps, the first-rate cricketer has achieved the more perfect performance : he has met every difficulty splendidly, his judgment as to running has been impeccable, he has not given a single chance. The writer, on the other hand, is—I think we may say—never perfect : consider those last chapters of " Don Quixote " ; consider Steerforth and that infernal . . . woman, Agnes ; the Grandfather and Little Nell. Yet the man of the book has traversed such an infinitely wider region than the man of the bat and ball : he has perhaps rectified the work of the Creator and made himself anew and made himself much better ; and so he has worked with all the world, fashioning a new life, discovering wonders where before there were no wonders, shewing secrets that had been hidden from the foundation of things, peering now and again, as Poe and Hawthorne peered, into the places of thick darkness, and, above all, voyaging into the unknown, perpetually climbing the steep white track that vanishes over the hill.

## Chapter VI

WE are, I think, in the period 1890–1900; or, perhaps, to be more accurate, let us say 1889–1899. Between these dates I made a translation of " Le Moyen de Parvenir," an early seventeenth-century book by an odd follower of Rabelais. I wrote " The Great God Pan," " The Inmost Light," " The Three Impostors," " The Hill of Dreams," a short collection of experiments called " Ornaments in Jade," " Hieroglyphics," " The White People," the first part of " A Fragment of Life," and " The Red Hand." As I have said, I had inherited a little capital and spent it, and at ample leisure wrote these books and tales, instead of doing honest work. In the words of some character in " The Three Impostors," I regarded my various legacies as an endowment of research.

Now, as to the first title on this list, I was inspired to translate " Le Moyen de Parvenir " by that earlier Rabelaisian enthusiasm, which had lasted on. I found the book (in the original edition, I think), a little dumpy volume, while I was in the employment of a firm of second-hand booksellers who lived not far from Leicester Square. I have been called a modest man in an after-dinner speech, and I hope I am one; but I am sure I was modest in 1888. For, finding that I could not get a " rise " on the £60 a year which York Street afforded me, I tried Leicester Square and asked as much as £80; thirty shillings a week. I think the firm were amused; but they gave it me, and I set about cataloguing books for them.

I did this under odd conditions. When I made my application, the Brothers—let us say—took me down to the place in the basement where my work would have to be done. Once, I suppose, it had been the underground back-kitchen of the house. The kitchen was occupied by two other employees of the firm. One of them kept the accounts; the other treated " foxed " plates and pages in baths and made them fresh again, and " grangerised " and packed up books that had been bought. And the kitchen had the illumination from the solid glass over which people walked as they passed the shop, and some sort of air from the outer world. But my workshop had neither one nor the other. Save for gas, it was in total darkness. Its air was dead. And the House asked me very fairly whether I thought I could stand it. I said I could, and so I went to work.

I was never any good at cataloguing, real, technical cataloguing. I was explaining the other day to a friend of mine, a most accomplished and learned cataloguer, how I despised his work. " This business," I said, " of putting little slanty lines between the words of a title-page. A pitiable job," I proceeded, " it must be so since I could never make anything of it." But, the truth is, I never had any heart for the work. I don't care twopence whether a book is in the first edition or in the tenth; nay, if the tenth is the best edition, I would rather have it. To me it appears mere childishness to consider whether Lowndes—I think that is one of the authorities—has seen three copies of some particular book or three hundred; the only question being: is the book worth reading or not? Then, when it comes to measuring an Elzevir, say, with a graduated rule, and pronouncing a little book three inches and a half high to be a "tall copy," my common sense revolts. In other words, I am sure that Bibliography is a capital game, but it is not my game. I disliked my work of cataloguing; but I loathed another branch of my work, that was indexing. Everybody knows about "grangerising." You take a book, say, Smith's "Life of Nollekens." In it many eighteenth-century personages are mentioned, and many London streets and public places. The indexer has to read through the book, noting every person, every place, and compile an index. And on this index the grangeriser, the bookseller, goes to work hunting his stock of plates, hunting certain well-known sources for pictures with which he can stuff the original work. He will destroy a dozen or a hundred or a thousand other books of less value to produce a kind of monster: "The Life of Nollekens," by Joseph Smith, 1 vol., 8vo., 17—. Enlarged to 3 vols. quarto, and furnished with 250 extra illustrations, comprising portraits, views, plans, maps, and original and facsimile letters from Blank, Dash, Chose, and other famous persons of the period. Purple Levant Morocco Jansenist;

in watered purple silk case, gilt. Price: A great deal."

There. I am afraid I have forgotten the trick of the business and my friend the expert cataloguer will say that it is a good thing indeed that I have changed my trade; but it is something like that. Well, indexing is a horrible job; a weariness, a nuisance; a matter of covering the table with innumerable little slips of paper that flow over on to the floor; and one must be careful and accurate, and I have always hated being careful, and accurate —unless I happen to be interested in what I am doing. Besides, I hold that " grangerising " is both barbarous and silly. So I didn't like my work, but I liked the Brothers. They were always most courteous. Near our establishment was a shop where a very old gentleman sold precious things. His shop windows were made of small squares of glass. Above them was an inscription to the effect that the firm were " Goldsmiths and Silversmiths to Their Majesties the King and Queen and to Her Royal Highness the Duchess of Kent." And the old gentleman who kept this shop wore what we call evening-dress all day long, and advanced to meet his customers with an inclined head, his hands clasped together. The Brothers were a good deal younger, but they were of the same school. They had a way of putting things. For example, Brother Charles was trying to teach me how to catalogue their very beautiful collection of French eighteenth-century illustrated books, the sort of books that have illustrations by Fragonard.

"And if, Mr. Machen," said Brother Charles,

"if it strikes you that any of these plates are brilliant impressions—well, we have no objection to your saying so."

It may be mentioned that the firm dealt occasionally in works which would not be suitable for the "center table" of a New England parlour. For themselves, for their own private taste, they read George Eliot and thought her by far the greatest novelist that the English Nation had ever produced. I am sure that they would have held "Peregrine Pickle"—save in the rare first impression—to be a low book, and Dickens, I conjecture, would have struck them as funny and vulgar. But, still, selling books was their business, and it was not their affair as booksellers to censor the morals of the works they sold. They dealt in rare books.

Well, one morning as I walked down from Great Russell Street to the shop, I was reading of the trial and conviction of a minor bookseller of Charing Cross Road. This Mr. Jackson, or whatever his name was, had been found guilty of selling obscene books, and had been sent to gaol, for nine months, if I remember. I mentioned the matter to Brother Ned as I entered.

"You've seen about Jackson?" I said.

"Yes, Mr. Machen," said Brother Ned, with a certain moral austerity of demeanour that was new to me. "We *have* seen about Mr. Jackson, and we wish to state at once that we have no sympathy with Mr. Jackson; none whatever. There is a *right* way, Mr. Machen, of doing these things and a *wrong* way."

Mr. Jackson, I may say, did not deal in rare books.

His prices were low, he appealed to the general public. I hasten to add that on the whole I sympathise with the Brothers on this matter. And I add also: that after more recent experiences of mine I am very loath to find fault with any persons who treat those in their employment as human beings, with the decent civilities, courtesies and considerations that are befitting between man and man. In those days I had no knowledge of the anthropoids; still, I appreciated the pleasant treatment I received.

Yet, with all their pleasant manners, I am afraid that the Brothers did not find in me the ideal cataloguer. Anyhow, one day Brother Ned came down to my darksome place with a queer little quarto in his hand, a quarto in a dull paper wrapper. He had it open, marked with a slip of paper, at a certain page, and so far as I remember, without any particular preface or explanation, he asked me to begin making a translation of the work from that point. I said: "Certainly, Mr. Edward," and began to translate without more ado.

And here I may say that my career as a French translator has always struck me as highly humorous. At the good old grammar school where I was educated and educated very well, I think that the headmaster thoroughly agreed with the boys that Foreign Languages were a silly game that, for various reasons, one had to play. Education was Latin and Greek, but a notion had arisen in these late days that one ought to learn French, and so there was a French master. But he wore neither cap nor gown, and so he was not a real master, and so, again, his language was not a real language. Therefore: poor M. Ménard! And I am afraid that he was a very bad master. If his authority had been supported, and if we had tried our best, I do not think we should have learned much; as it was, the French lessons, three times a week, were a farce. I knew no French when I left Hereford Cathedral School in 1880, that is, I could not have conjugated the verb *Aimer* to save my life. I had read no French to speak of. Then, in my desolation in Clarendon Road, I had somehow come across "Gil Blas" and had managed, being interested, to get through it. Then, the York Street publisher had sent me down the sixteenth-century "Heptameron" and had ordered me to translate it, and I did so, somehow. And now, Brother Ned ordered me to translate from the dumpy quarto which he handed me; and forthwith I set about translating, not troubling what it was, what it was about, not caring two straws that I had not the thread of the narrative, nor worrying over the fact that I knew nothing whatever about the enigmatic "M.M." or the mysterious "C.C." into whose singular adventures I now plunged gaily. Thus I began the translation of the famous "Memoirs of Casanova," and I think the money balance between the Brothers and myself was readjusted. For if I had been dear as a cataloguer, at thirty shillings a week, I was decidedly cheap as a translator. Casanova is a work that runs into twelve sizeable volumes, and the task of turning it into English took me a year, and I think the cost to the firm will be held to have been strictly moderate.

## Things Near and Far

And what about these strange Memoirs of the charlatan adventurer? Well, not long ago I was called upon to write an introduction to a reissue of the version I had made in the 'eighties. I found this an extremely difficult task. The obvious solution of the difficulty, the writing a sort of *précis* of the book and calling it an Introduction, did not appeal to me. It was some time before the "moral" of the Memoirs disengaged itself. The Introduction when written proved to be an essay on the futility of trying to tell the whole truth about the relations between men and women. This is what Casanova, who was highly qualified, in a certain sense, for the undertaking, tried to do; and the more "frank," the more "outspoken" his page the more the secret escapes from it; the more openly he reveals, the more deeply he conceals the mysteries. For the fact is that all the real secrets are ineffable; the secrets of love, and the secrets of the wood; the secrets of the flower and the secrets of the flame; and the secrets of the Faith. As I point out in my Introduction, you can enumerate the scientific facts—such of them as are known—relating to any subject. You can define a horse, for example, as Bitzer defined it in "Hard Times."

"Quadruped. Graminivorous. Forty teeth, namely twenty-four grinders, four eye-teeth and twelve incisive. Sheds coat in the spring; in marshy countries sheds hoofs, too. Hoofs hard, but requiring to be shod with iron. Age known by marks in mouth."

And so you may discourse of the pistils and stamens of the lilies of the field, and divide the fowls of the air into genera and species and subspecies and count the teeth of Keats: and when all is done, you know—nothing. Nothing that is of the essence of your matter, nothing of its "quiddity," a word that we have ceased to use, I suppose, because we have no use for it, having forgotten that there is such a thing as that essence which is present in all things, which indeed makes them to be what they are, which is nevertheless unsearchable and ineffable. And all this is true, not only of the matters which the plain man, the man in the street, is inclined to sniff at, but of all things, of man himself and of the universe of noumena and phenomena which is presented to him. If you talk to the plain, practical man about Mystic Theology, Mystic Love, Poetry, Romance, he will, very likely, brush you aside with his "In my opinion that's all imagination"—and serve you right for talking to him on such subjects at all. The dear fellow has no notion of the fact that he has never seen a point, a line, a square, or a triangle, and that he never will see any one of these things—in this life at all events. He has seen black marks on paper which he has been told are lines and squares and triangles. Being at heart thoroughly credulous, he believes what he is told, but if he will dig up his old "Euclid" and read the definitions, he will find that no mortal eyes can ever see a square or a circle, since a line is length without breadth and a plane surface is length and breadth without thickness. There is nothing in the nature of things to prevent a man from seeing a dragon or a griffin, a gorgon or a unicorn. Nobody as a matter of fact has seen a woman whose hair consisted of snakes, nor a horse from whose forehead a horn projected; though very early man most probably did see dragons—known to science as pterodactyls—and monsters more improbable than griffins. At any rate, none of these zoological fancies violates the fundamental laws of the intellect; the monsters of heraldry and mythology do not exist, but there is no reason in the nature of things nor in the laws of the mind why they should not exist. But no man hath seen a line at any time, since the manifestation of length without breadth is a contradiction in terms. And the plain man is probably inclined to believe in the existence of vulgar fractions; he may tell you that he makes use of them daily in his calculations. But let him study the story of the race between Achilles and the Tortoise, and note to what monstrous results his belief in elementary arithmetic inevitably conducts him; results which are more intolerable than a madman's dreams.

And then, again, there are wider, more universal conceptions than anything contained in the geometry and arithmetic books. In a little book of mine with the bad title of "War and the Christian Faith"—the publisher chose the title—I speak thus of Space and Time:

"Take two insistent and unavoidable examples (of the things which are unsearchable and indefinable), space and time. No man who strolls from his arm-chair to the mantelpiece and watches the hands of the clock move round can deny the

## Things Near and Far

existence of either, since he has walked from point to point in one and seen the other measured before his eyes. But as to understanding space and time, what highest philosophy can attain to such a pitch? The limitless cannot so much as be imagined in the mind, nor imagined in a nightmare: but that space which you have traversed of some eight or ten feet is limitless, and must be so.

"It is a sea without a shore. And time, that which your two-guinea clock ticks off for you, as you watch the dial: it had no beginning that you can picture; it can have no end save with God. You cannot understand; you must believe; and so on your very hearth-rug the infinites and eternities are before you and confront you, as truly as the clock face confronts you."

And the conclusion of the whole matter is that we live and move in a world of profound and ineffable mystery; that all things from the most abstract to the most concrete are involved in this mystery, and, *therefore*, that Casanova as an exponent of love is a futile fellow. He was a Voltairean; he approached the question as he would say without prejudices, as the foolish among us would say, without any nonsense, or, as the still more foolish among us would say, in a scientific spirit. And the result is exactly what might be expected: nothing. Love is defined and expounded in the spirit of Bitzer defining a horse; and one perceives that science misapplied is just gibberish, nothing more or less. Otherwise, taking Casanova's

Memoirs from a lower standpoint, they are in many places vastly entertaining. He knew all Europe from Petersburg and Constantinople to London and Madrid; he was familiar with the palace and the gutter; he was the friend of Kings and philosophers and popes—and also of the scum of the eighteenth-century earth. One cannot understand the period as a whole without knowing Casanova.

So I translated and translated day after day; but in a few months' time the black hole in which I worked began very violently to disagree with me. I got ill, and it was clear that some change must be made. The Brothers, as always, were courteous and considerate: why not do the work at home? I assented very willingly, worked at the task for five hours every day, and every Saturday took my parcel of copy to the shop and got my thirty shillings, the week's wages.

And here I must make a boast, which is not wholly a boast: the second part of this sentence I shall explain no farther. I finished the translation of the Memoirs, but the book was not immediately issued. On the completion of my job the Brothers needed me no more. I imagine that they wanted a real, expert, technical cataloguer, not a literary man of sorts; and my having worked for them for some months at my own home and not in the shop made it easy for them to get rid of me quietly; rather, to let me fade away, without the least suspicion of firmness, much less of harshness. And they were always very glad to see me when I chose to look them up, either on business or merely as a friendly caller. I remember, for example, that when I had finished the translation of "Le Moyen de Parvenir" and was "subscribing" the book with "the trade," I called at the shop and was received with a genial and kindly courtesy that I have not forgotten, though it is a long time since 1890; but then I do not forget. And lest it should be suspected by some persons that under a veil of benignity I am "getting at" the Brothers all the time, I hasten to say that this is not so; to say this in the strongest manner possible. True, thirty shillings a week was not good pay for decent French-English translating, even in 1889; but it was the wages that I had asked myself, having been thoroughly convinced by my experiences of the six preceding years that I was such a dismal and incapable ass that if I just managed to escape the Governorship of the Island of Farre Joyaunce—otherwise the ditch or the workhouse—it was as much as I could expect. So I asked my thirty shillings a week and hoped in my heart that it was not too much; and I am not blaming the Brothers in the least because they did not press more upon me. And, however that may be, they were always courteous and kindly in all communications that passed between us; and for that they shall be in my grateful memory so long as I live. I have said already, I think, how once during the last year of my employment on the "Evening News," finding myself in old haunts of long ago, Wellington Street, Bow Street, York Street, anguish possessed me as I remembered how I had once starved and had known something like happiness while I toiled over the ancient occult books in the Catherine Street garret;

anguish possessed me as I recollected the happy time in misery. And, as I said to a friend soon afterwards: "In those days I was getting considerably less money in a whole year than I am now getting in a month; and yet..."

Again, I say, if our clergy would but mind their business. If instead of enquiring into the exact cut of bodices, instead of passing anxious hours as to the pernicious corruptions of the Fox-Trot and the Bunny Hug, instead of working with all their hearts and souls to make sure that no one can possibly get a glass of bitter beer after ten o'clock, instead of unmasking the inferno of the race-course, the utter levity of much of our railway literature; if, instead of all this accursed drivel, cant and imbecility, they would but say Mass and preach the Gospel, and otherwise quite abide in peace! Let them go to the Book, and there they will find that the most horrible sin denounced in it is neither gambling, drinking nor wantoning, but the sin of shaming a man, of bitterly insulting him, of making him mean in his own eyes, of making him despise his own self as something unutterably fouled and scorned and bewrayed. What is the text? Something like: but he that sayeth to his brother, "Thou fool," shall be in danger of hell fire.

I am drawing a contrast between 1889 and 1921, and hence I say that the Brothers always treated me with the common decency due from one human being to another, though they were rich and I was poor, though they were men of business and I an idiot in all matters of business, though they were masters and I was man.

## Things Near and Far

And now as to the famous boast. As I said, I ceased to be in the employment of these good men. I went into the country, up on the Chiltern Hills. We neither saw nor heard anything of each other. But all the while those legacies of which I have spoken came dropping slow, and in 1893, when I had made up my mind to return to London, I think I must have had in bank something between three and four thousand pounds. I was assailed by an unworthy pang of prudence, by one of the foolish notions that the world's people take for wisdom. It struck me that this living on capital, taking the pieces of eight by fistfuls out of the chest, would never do; that the money ought to be invested, preferably in some business in which I could contribute work as well as money. I looked about me, I advertised, I saw some people in the City and found nothing promising from my point of view, though I found here and there such curiosities as London, I believe, only affords. For example, in a very dim sort of cock-loft in an old house in the heart of the City, I hit upon a firm of general agents who had answered my advertisement. There were two of them: one, a young, rosy, out-in-the-open sort of man, the other elderly, frock-coated, with a kind of dissenting beard on his chin. He talked of the version of Horace's odes that he was shortly bringing out at his own expense, and discussed with me the true pronunciation of the Latin language with much intelligence. The junior partner's talk was of trawling, and indeed he said that the firm was a sort of trawling concern—in City waters.

But nothing came of it, and at last I bethought me of the Brothers. Brother Charles was as genial as ever. He saw my point. He said: "We are going to issue Casanova at last; why not put a thousand pounds into that for a start?" I agreed, and the matter was settled. And then, very nervously, with a good deal of hesitation, with a certain difficulty in the choice of words, Brother Charles said:

"Of course, Mr. Machen, we quite recognise the ... er ... circumstances in which you made your most admirable translation of the book. It was ... er ... in a manner ... er ... task-work; yes, *task-work*. Well ... the case is now, to a certain degree ... altered; you have an interest in the prosperity of the venture, and, in short, we rather wondered whether you would like to ... to ... *revise* your manuscript."

"Mr. Charles," I replied, "I did the job as well as I could; and I don't think I can make it any better."

## Chapter VII

BEROALDE DE VERVILLE proved to be what the elder members of the theatrical profession used to call " a pill." Only the other day I was reading a French account of this author. The critic said in the course of his remarks that many people who had gone to the " Moyen de Parvenir " in search of unpleasantness had turned back from the quest, deterred by the difficulty of the language. And I don't know that it is more difficult for a modern Frenchman than for an Englishman. It is written in a sort of Babylonish dialect which is not exactly French though it looks like it ; as Meredith looks like English to the casual glance. And then, it is not only difficult, but obscure ; not only are the sentences queerly constructed, but the subject-matter is of a highly dubious and cloudy character : when you have found out what Beroalde is saying, you begin to wonder what he is saying it about. And, then, there are bits of old dialect peppered about this excessively odd volume. I remember coming upon two words : " iquent hesne." I sat down in front of them, and looked at them from every angle. I don't know how I found out at last that " iquent hesne " was a sort of seventeenth-century French " Zummerzet " for " cette chêne " —" thicky oāk." Again the " Moyen " is thick with puns, of the kind that used to be called in the golden days of Burlesque " outrageous " : and the time I wasted in trying to turn these silly French tricks into sillier English contortions! On the whole, I would say that " Le Moyen de Parvenir " in literature is as a cathedral constructed entirely of gargoyles would be in architecture. Rabelais is full of gargoyles, " apes and owls and antics," as he calls them, on the outside of the jar. But within, as he rightly claims, there are precious medicines, aromatic balms of singular power and virtue. And so far as I can judge, Beroalde is all oddity and nothing else. He cost me a year's hard labour; the version was issued and is now valued by collectors; and that is all that need be said.

And now—in 1890—I began to try a little journalism of the more or less literary kind. I began, I think, by writing " Turnovers " for the " Globe," and miscellaneous articles for the " St. James's Gazette," and at length stories for the latter paper, which was then edited by Mr.—now Sir—Sydney Lowe. The " Globe " is extinct, the " St. James's Gazette " is merged and submerged in the " Evening Standard "; there are no papers of such metal now in existence. The difference between them and the evening papers of the day is a very simple one: the former were meant to please the educated, the latter are designed to entertain the uneducated, and the uneducated may be equated, very largely indeed, with women. It is an odd paradox: there is no doubt, I suppose, that the instruction—or, if you like, education—of women has made immense strides in the last thirty years; and yet it is true that when a newspaper editor says to himself: "We have an immense number of women readers and we must see that they get what they like," the result is drivel. This sort of thing:

> Madame has just discovered a new craze. Jewelled clay pipes and shag tobacco delicately sprinkled with gold-dust are now quite *démodés* when once we cross the borders of Balham; but my lady prides herself on her collection of hookahs, the water-pipes of the gorgeous East.
>
> It is quite the thing, I hear, amongst really smart women to give "Hookah Teas." Everybody wears Oriental costume, and sits on cushions piled on the floor, and delicately draws in the aroma of the rarest Turkish Tobacco, scented by its passage through rosewater or lavender-water. At Lady Clarinda Belsize's Hookah Tea last Wednesday, two native musicians played the tom-tom and the *guzla* behind a curtain, or *purdah*, as I am told it is called. Of course *yashmaks* were worn by all the guests.

There; it is not worth parodying. And there is another sort of terrible tosh which deals with the doings of "The Summer Girl" and "The Winter Girl" and "The Marathon Girl": all of it a very feeble imitation of the cheapest American journalism. In the 'nineties this kind of thing existed, but it was confined to the columns of one or two ladies' papers. In those days, I would not say that the editors of evening papers brought out their journals exclusively for the benefit of the members of the best clubs of St. James's and Pall Mall; but I certainly should say that they had the clubs in their mind's eye; that they presumed a certain standard of education and culture in their readers. All that ended when the evening "Westminster Gazette" came to an end.

But indeed there would be little harm done if a column or two columns or three columns were reserved for the "Hookah Tea" stuff and the "Caravan Girl" stuff and all similar stuff. You could skip these columns if you didn't like them, just as I skip the racing columns, in which I am not interested. But "the women" rule the whole paper. Not only must the editor put in matter which he knows they will like, he must keep out matter which he knows they won't like. And the result is . . . the result as we know it. As the "literary editor" of a big London paper acutely observed to me not long ago, the case of the newspaper article is exactly as the case of chops and steaks, beefsteak puddings and saddles of mutton that were of old. "The women" have spoilt all. What do they know or care about man's food? To them there is nothing to choose between a chop fried white and hard and greasy in the frying-pan and a chop which has been purged of all excess by the ardent heat beneath the gridiron, which beneath a coat half black, half golden-brown, preserves its delicious juices, which sizzles on the plate as William or Charles serves it, which, opened by the eager knife, shews within a hue like that of a blush-rose in June. These are not matters to enchant the wayward heart of a young girl, and when once she sets foot inside the tavern coffee-room, farewell to all such solid merits. There was once a noble tavern called Herbert's, famous for two generations. Men who had spent half a lifetime in Africa or India or in the islands of the South Seas were sustained by the thought of the beefsteak pudding at Herbert's. The times changed and the old tavern with them. Going there in these later days, I used to wonder why all the meats seemed to taste alike, why there was no distinctive and peculiar relish about any of the dishes. I found out the reason why one day. I had business, oddly enough, in Herbert's kitchen. One of the cooks shewed me the joints roasting on the jack; and I perceived that three different meats were cooking at the one fire, while beneath, in a common pan, their juices mingled, ready for the basting ladle. It is not much wonder, I think, that veal and lamb and beef taste all much alike in this unhappy place, once so high, now fallen so low. One night I was dining there, and a member of the party asked the waiter to bring him some Stilton. " I beg your pardon, sir," said the man, " we only have *English* cheeses." It sounds impossible; but I heard this with my ears. In the old days Herbert's was exclusively masculine in its custom; I do not know what would have happened to that waiter then. I hardly think that his death would have been an easy one.

But to " the women " all this is of no account. They know nothing about man's food, as I say, and they care less. I do not blame them; I do not blame myself for being ignorant of the difference between Hopsac and Gaberdine: but how would *they* like it if I poked my nose into their Oxford Street shops and insisted on these shops being carried on to suit my taste?

So through this monstrous incursion of women, with the war and the nursery hours of to-day, the old tavern life has gone; utterly and for ever, I am afraid. A good thing has gone. The old mahogany boxes with bright brass work and green curtains, the light twinkling in the dark polished surfaces that were all about the room, the flaming fire with the plates warming by it, the plain food, the best of its kind, cooked in the best possible manner, the mighty tankards of mighty ale, the port that *was* port afterwards, in itself a great gift and a curious grace, and later—say about eleven o'clock—Charles appearing with a large china bowl and a bottle under his arm, following up these things with lump sugar, lemons, and the hot water: it is all over. And it is not only the good material things that have been taken away: the good meats and the good drinks, the glowing mahogany and the cheerful blaze and crackle of the fire: with them has gone, I suspect, a certain genial habit of the mind and soul which was congruous with all the circumstances of the old-fashioned tavern, which was congruous also with good men and good books and choice poetry, with all the rich zest and relish and unction which made the Victorian age of letters a great age; and, in its measure, a worthy successor to three other illustrious tavern ages: the Shakespearian, the Caroline, and the Johnsonian. Think of Falstaff and his tavern bill and his warning against thin potations, think of Herrick and his address to Ben, his fond remembrance of the taverns "where we such clusters had as made us nobly wild not mad," think of Johnson squeezing the orange into the bowl with antick gestures, saying " Who's for *poonsh?* " think of Tennyson and that blest pint of port at the vanished Cock Tavern, think of Dickens, that great lover of tavern feasts and immortaliser of them : think of all this, my poor young man, and beat your breast. There are no jolly taverns for you, and your favourite authors do not write like men—" my son Cartwright writes all like a man," said Ben Jonson—but like psycho-analytical chemists.

And as I was saying, as with the taverns, so with the papers. When I wrote a little for them, in 1890 or thereabouts, it was allowable to assume a certain amount of literacy, a certain knowledge in the reader. Now that is over. I know the case of a man who, I am certain, pretends ignorance that he may continue to be employed. As it happens, he is an expert in food and drink ; but I have known him number Beaujolais with the wines of Bordeaux in a newspaper article, and speak of curry powder and pickles as ordinary ingredients in veal and ham pie. I believe he knows much better ; but he has probably found out that a misstatement or two gives an easy careless air that is much admired. Nobody can call a writer of this kind a pedant. A highly accomplished journalist said to me a few years ago : " Always remember that we appeal, not to the cabman, but to the cabman's wife." And another instance, though I am afraid it is somewhat tinged with self-praise. I had written a brief article for the " Evening News " on a topic that had been given to me; I was to explain *why* it is that a " mean street " of to-day is, generally, hideous and appalling, while a row of sixteenth-century cottages is, generally, a delight to see. I did as I always do when I can, I took the particular instance and placed it under a general principle. I said the chief horror of the modern street was not to be sought in the poverty of the design, though that was, doubtless, bad enough, but in the fact that in the street of to-day each house is a replica of the other, so that the effect to the eye is, if the street be long enough, the prolongation of one house to infinity, in an endless series of repetitions. And I pointed out that even if you admired some particular picture or statue immensely, it would be rather awful to traverse a long gallery in which the picture or the statue were repeated again and again as far as the eye could see. And then, on the other hand, I shewed how the sixteenth-century cottages were each of them individuals, each with some slight difference from the cottage next door, each with its variety in door or window or pent-house. And hence, I urged, a continual slight surprise to the beholder, and taking the supposed row as a whole, that strangeness in the proportion which Bacon declared, most profoundly, to be necessary to the highest beauty. Well, I got this with difficulty into the prescribed 500 words—" nobody will read anything over 500 words "—and said to myself : " Now that Patmore is dead, nobody else could have written that article. But . . . there will be a row." There was. Lord Northcliffe gave the little essay the honour of a special mention in one of his famous *communiqués*—as I believe they were called. He spoke of it with venom as "a wiseacre article." I am sure he was perfectly right from his point of view. The fault was mine. " When I am in Rome, I fast on Saturdays," said one of the Fathers.

Things have changed indeed. I was mentioning Coventry Patmore. In the Introduction to the " Religio Poetæ," a collection of short essays of the profoundest wisdom, he acknowledges his obligations to Greenwood, once editor of the " St. James's Gazette." Some of these essays had appeared in that journal : the fact is quite stupefying considered in the light of the journalism of to-day. Education increases ; ignorance grows deeper.

Let me not be understood as claiming that my newspaper work of thirty-two years ago was characterised by the profoundest wisdom. Very far from it ; my articles were harmless and agreeable enough, I think, in a small way ; and writing them, I first began to get a hint of my true subject ; the country of my childhood and my youth. And I thus began to move away from the exotic Rabelaisian influence, both as to manner and to matter : to perceive that not the splendid Loire but the humble Soar brook, winding and shining in deep valleys and obscured by dark alder thickets, was my native stream. I began to see that I was a citizen of Caerleon-on-Usk, and not of Tours or of Chinon, and that the old grey manor-houses and the white farms of Gwent had their beauty and significance, though they were not castles in Touraine. There was something of all this, of course, in " The Chronicle of Clemendy," the Great Romance which was neither great nor a romance; but in this everything was viewed and everything expressed in an exotic medium : now I saw that a blossoming thorn bush in the valley of the Soar and the nightingale singing in it and the river level about Caerleon and the red fires of sunset over the mountain in the west were all in themselves and by themselves fit matter for the work; that they needed not to be disguised in a French literary habit of four hundred years ago.

It was in this summer of 1890 that I wrote the first chapter of " The Great God Pan." I have told the whole story in the Introduction to the latest edition of that fantasy, which is published by Messrs. Simpkin, Marshall, and whether I should weary my readers I know not, but I do know that I should weary myself if I told it all over again. The tale was written in bits, in the intervals between severe literary cramps, as I have mentioned in this present volume, and it was published by Mr. John Lane, of the Bodley Head, at the end of 1894, when yellow bookery was at its yellowest. And it aroused a certain amount of attention. There was a storm —in a doll's teacup.

The other day a friend of mine said genially to me:

" I have just been reading that 'Great God Pan' of yours over again, and I really don't see that there's much in it to make a sensation of."

I am sure he was quite right. But a sensation there was, of a minor kind. It had some mysterious property in it, this little book, which caused good

*Things Near and Far*

men to froth at the mouth, greatly to my delight. I have quoted a good many of the reviews in the Introduction to the Simpkin, Marshall edition: things like this:

" We are afraid he only succeeds in being ridiculous. The book is, on the whole, the most acutely and intentionally disagreeable we have yet seen in English. We could say more, but refrain from doing so for fear of giving such a work advertisement."—" Manchester Guardian."

" This book is gruesome, ghastly, and dull . . . the majority of readers will turn from it in utter disgust."—" Lady's Pictorial."

" These tricks have also their ludicrous side." —" Guardian."

And so forth. It is very well, but I cannot help saying, as an old craftsman and an old reviewer, that it might have been better. I have no fault to find with the technique of the " Guardian " ; but the " Lady's Pictorial " should have left out the " gruesome " and the " ghastly " and also, I am inclined to think, the "disgust." There are readers who like the gruesome and the ghastly; there are readers whose curiosity is stimulated by the term " disgust." I am afraid, for example, that if the account of legal proceedings, civil or criminal, is headed " Disgusting Details," there are minds so prurient as to be rather attracted than repelled, and I am sure that the gentle scribe of the " Lady's Pictorial " did not wish to paint my little book in attractive colours. And so with the " Manchester Guardian." " Ridiculous" is admirable; but "acutely and intentionally disagreeable" is something of a signal set to attract those prurient readers whose existence I have regretted; and the last sentence says too much. Mr. Harry Quilter, something of a figure in those days, did better. He pointed out in an article in the "Contemporary Review"—also something of a figure in those days—that the only explanation he could give of such favourable notices as the book had received was that the author must have a great many friends engaged in journalism. I wrote a temperate letter to Mr. Quilter in which I said I was very sorry, but I didn't know any journalists at all—which happened to be the truth. He wrote back to remind me, as he said, that there was "an Inmost Light to which you may yet be true"—"The Inmost Light" is the title of a tale which was included in the first edition of "The Great God Pan."

—One of the saddest books in the world is Mrs. Gaskell's wonderful "Life of Charlotte Brontë." But there is one tragi-comical touch. Poor valiant, simple, stricken Charlotte was being entertained in town by Mr. and Mrs. Smith. There was a dinner-party, given, I suppose, in her honour, and she writes to an old friend:

"There were only seven gentlemen at dinner besides Mr. Smith, but of these five were critics—men more dreaded in the world of letters than you can conceive. I did not know how much their presence and conversation had excited me till they were gone, and the reaction commenced. When I had retired for the night, I wished to sleep—the

*Things Near and Far*

effort to do so was vain. I could not close my eyes. Night passed; morning came, and I rose without having known a moment's slumber."

Who were these terrible five? We do not know, and it is possible enough that if we heard their names we should not have heard of their names, though, likely enough, George Henry Lewes was one of them. It is odd and pathetic too to think that a great woman such as Charlotte Brontë should have allowed the brilliant repartees and tremendous reputation of George Henry Lewes to break her rest. And just before this passage there is another, as strange and as pathetic. A severe review of " Shirley " appeared in " The Times." Mr. and Mrs. Smith kindly " mislaid " the paper. But Charlotte insisted on pressing the thorn to her bosom. She would see " The Times."

"Mrs. Smith took her work, and tried not to observe the countenance, which the other tried to hide between the huge sheets; but she could not help becoming aware of tears stealing down the face and dropping on the lap."

And all over a review, an unfavourable review! It is very strange, or, at least, it seems so to me, since, like Jim the nigger, I don't never cry ska'sely over reviews, and I have always contrived to get my usual sleep.

But I have left out one curious specimen of the " Great God Pan " reviews, a specimen which leads up to a curious passage. The " Westminster Review " said:

" It is an incoherent nightmare of sex and the

supposed horrible mysteries behind it, such as might conceivably possess a man who was given to a morbid brooding over these matters, but which would soon lead to insanity if unrestrained ... innocuous from its absurdity."

I was talking over old literary doings and the affairs of the 'nineties with a friend one day in the spring of 1921. My friend was asking me about my early books and their reception. I gave him a lurid account of the castigations which I had received on account of " The Great God Pan."

"Why," said I, " the ' Westminster ' practically told me that if I didn't take care I should end up in a lunatic asylum."

" Well," replied the man, meaning to be funny, " haven't you ? I understood you were at Carmelite House ? "

" No," I returned, also meaning to be funny, " I haven't. All the lunatic asylums that I've heard of have been managed by a *doctor*."

During the latter part of my stay in the country (1891–93) I wrote two books. I have forgotten the names of both of them. They were very bad, and I tore them up, with the exception of one episode —to put it mildly, not a very good story—which appears in " The Three Impostors " under the title of " The Novel of the Dark Valley." And it was in the early spring of 1894 that I set about the writing of the said " Three Impostors," a book which testifies to the vast respect I entertained for the fantastic, " New Arabian Nights " manner of R. L.

Stevenson, to those curious researches in the byways of London which I have described already, and also, I hope, to a certain originality of experiment in the tale of terror, as exemplified in the stories of the Professor who was taken by the fairies, and of the young student of law who swallowed the White Powder. And when I had finished, with a sort of recognition that I had squeezed this particular orange to death, I remember saying to my old friend A. E. Waite : " I shall never give anybody a White Powder again." And then I was immediately called on to do that very thing which I had vowed I would not do. I actually got an " order," and—this shews that I was a mere intruder, not a true craftsman— I have rarely been so miserable, miserable that is, as a man of letters, in my life.

It was like this. As I have remarked, " The Great God Pan " had made a storm in a Tiny Tot's teacup. And about the same time, a young gentleman named H. G. Wells had made a very real, and a most deserved sensation with a book called " The Time Machine " ; a book indeed. And a new weekly paper was projected by Mr. Raven Hill and Mr. Girdlestone, a paper that was to be called " The Unicorn." And both Mr. Wells and myself were asked to contribute ; I was to do a series of horror stories. I won't deny that I swelled a little and was cheered and elated by the fact of my being asked to write by anybody ; nay, I really tried my best to feel important and puffed up. And then I set about writing that series of tales of horror. I was not puffed up for long. As I say, I had realised that for me the Stevensonian manner was ended.

## Things Near and Far

And now I was to begin all over again; to recook that cabbage which was already boiled to death! I wrote four stories in a kind of agony, my pen shrieking "rubbish!" at me with every stroke. I remember literally sobbing in a kind of hysteria of despair with my head on my hands; and this shews that there are some men who cannot be helped. The only thing that got me through at all was an endeavour to transplant the manner of Apuleius into English soil; but the four tales were sorry things when all was said. I was glad when "The Unicorn" ceased to exist after two or three numbers, before a single one of those tales of mine had appeared in it. Mr. Wells had one story in "The Unicorn," "The Cone," which he reprinted in the collection called "The Country of the Blind." Such was the affair, and I think it explains the irritation which I have always experienced when I have been asked to write a continuation of "The Three Impostors," or something in the manner of "The Three Impostors." I knew that all this was done and ended; that, for me, the vein was worked out and exhausted: utterly. I shall always recur to the metaphor of the white road that you see from afar climbing over the hill into unconjectured regions. For me that is literature; the journey of discovery; the finding of a new world. When once I have toiled painfully up that long road, and have stood on the other side of the dark wood, and have looked upon the land beyond; then all the joy, all the delight and thrill and wonder are over for me. Columbus could not discover America twice. I never can say to myself: "Look here! Let's pretend that we've never been this way before, that we don't know in the least what's beyond that turn of the road, that anything may happen beyond that pine tree." It won't do.

And that is one reason why I beg my bread in my sixtieth year.

For, all that I have written on this matter is, doubtless, very fine; but we must confess that when it is a case of literature being exchanged for the money of the publisher—and the public—the affair becomes a commercial one. And, in business, you buy a brand. Let me try to imagine it! I am a wealthy man, and I have found and my guests have found that last hamper of Champagne admirable. I go to my wine merchant and order another hamper of the same vintage. Nay, he has not got it; he will be happy to supply me with a wine of entirely different character; or, to press the analogy a little extravagantly, he no longer deals in Champagne at all, he doesn't think much of Champagne, it is an elegant lemonade, as one of Murger's characters expresses it, but he will be delighted to send me six dozen of a rare Château wine of Bordeaux, an infinitely finer wine, as he assures me. But I want Champagne! I am not going to stand such treatment for one moment! The man must be mad! *De me fabula narratur;* all my life I have been pressing my Bordeaux on people who had begun to think that there might be something to be said for my small Champagne.

And I quite see the point. I have never read one of the horror stories of Mr. W. W. Jacobs, though I am told that they are admirable. For me, Mr.

Jacobs must speak through an everlasting Night Watchman, through an eternal countryman draining the last dregs of his beer on the settle at the *Cauliflower :* with these immortals I am happy.

"The Three Impostors" was published by John Lane some time in 1895. But before sending the manuscript to Mr. Lane, I had tried Mr. Heinemann. The firm wrote me a most delightful letter, full of the most charming things, which I had some difficulty in swallowing, though an author's throat is capable of astounding feats where praise is concerned. I was to go and see them, and I did so, my heart beating high. I saw a member of the firm. He was better than the letter for a swelling soul. He read extracts from the reader's report, and these were more splendid still. He outlined delightful terms; he pressed on me the necessity of my having something on account of royalties in advance : a happy possibility that had not even dawned on me in 1894-95. He hoped that the House of Heinemann might ever have the privilege of publishing my beautiful books. "Better than the best of Stevenson"; thus he read from the optimistic reader's report. Thus elated, glorious, happy indeed, went down Mr. Arthur Machen, man of letters—now there could be no doubt of it !—from the amiable office, even into Bedford Street, seen for the first time to be a shining thoroughfare, a veritable golden pathway of Paradise, leading to the golden Strand, nay, to the golden world, where all desires were accomplished, and the faithful servant is rewarded : "Enter thou into the joy of thy Publisher."

## Things Near and Far

After all, I said to myself, the old toils, the old labours, those unhappy nights, those sick days of despair were not altogether wasted. Indeed, I tried to do my best; indeed, I grudged no labour; indeed, I was patient and tore up the sorry page; I knew that I must persevere and still persevere. And I knew that the other books were well meant but futile after all; that I had not really touched the mark, though I pretended that I had, and did my best to persuade myself that it was so. But now; " I have really written something that is good, that is, even, very good; that one of the best publishers in London praises and praises highly." I never thought of the money that all this must mean, that never entered a moment into my mind; my only meditation was that for fifteen years I had done all I could do, and that now I was to enter into my reward. O golden Strand, that day, golden Great Russell Street when I came home to tell my news, golden happy world which rewards at last all humble faithful endeavour: golden world inhabited by good men, by publishers of all men most good.

It was a pure matter of form; the waiting for the agreement, a matter of a week or so, as the kind gentlemen in the office informed me. And in three weeks, somewhere about the middle of January, 1895, came the MS. of " The Three Impostors " back to me, with a formal, printed slip from the House of Heinemann, regretting that it was unable to accept the enclosed manuscript. Well does A. E. Waite declare that there is an element of waggery in the constitution of the universe. Never did the proud policeman in the old pantomime, foiled by the buttered slide of the clown, come down with a thump so boisterously undignified. So, rolling in the mud, I lay sprawling, my legs in the air. I was silly enough to write a somewhat exasperated letter to my friend in the office. He answered me in a befitting manner, in a tone of grave rebuke: he said that if I had realised the cares of the publisher's life I would not have written " so caustically."

## Chapter VIII

"THE Three Impostors" came back then from Messrs. Heinemann, and as soon as I got over the little bump I have just mentioned, I thought that I would try to make the book a bit better. One of the "novels" or introduced tales displeased me, so I am sure it must have been very bad indeed. I am not certain, but I think it was about a benevolent City man, of considerable means, who occupied an old red brick house somewhere at the back of Acton and occasionally, I suppose at the full moon, turned into a were-wolf. I can see nothing against the plot; and I believe there is a considerable body of unimpeachable evidence in favour of the hypothesis that the human consciousness is occasionally displaced by the bestial consciousness: the Malays, for instance, are apt at times to fancy themselves wild cats and to behave accordingly. But, somehow, it wouldn't do. The transformation of the City man was highly unsatisfactory and unconvincing: so I tore up the tale, and wrote instead of it the surprising narrative of Professor Gregg and his disastrous search for the fairies among the hills of my native country. In the machinery of the story I introduced a hypothesis that was then new; I think I read of it in some paper written by Sir Oliver Lodge. The theory was, that when the

*Things Near and Far*

lights are low, or turned out, at the spiritualist séance, and objects are found, when the lights go up, to have been brought from all quarters of the room and laid in the centre of the table; or when the people sitting in the dark round the table hear the piano near the door being played, the theory was that these marvels are not necessarily due to the presence and intervention of ghosts. I believe that it was the case of Eusapia Palladino that was engaging Sir Oliver Lodge's attention just then; and he advanced the striking hypothesis that the piano was played and the objects fetched from the sideboard by a kind of extension of the medium's body. I forget whether the distinguished Professor used the instance; but I know that the impression conveyed to my mind was that something happened similar to the protrusion and withdrawal of a snail's horns: Eusapia's arm became twice or thrice its usual length, performed the required feat whatever it was, and then shrank again to its normal size. This hypothesis was novel in those days; now it is widely known and credited amongst spiritualists. They have found a name for the mysterious substance which projects itself from the medium's body: it is called ectoplasm. In all probability the whole theory is a pack of nonsense, and the "phenomena" are the tricks of clever cheats: still, what do we know? At all events, I worked it all into my fairy tale, mixing up the old view that the fairy tales, the stories of Little People, are in fact traditions of the aborigines of these islands, small, dark men who took refuge under the hills from the invading Celt with this view of the capacities of the human body, and my view, still newer, that the fairies may still be found under the hills, and that they are far from being pleasant little people. That was the recipe for the tale, and I give it in spite of a friendly rebuke I once received from poor H. B. Irving. He was talking to me about the Introduction I had written to "The Great God Pan."

"You shouldn't have done it," he said. "You destroy the illusion. Never take people behind the scenes. I never do."

But it really doesn't matter. And, further, I have a suspicion that it is often much more interesting " behind " than " in front." I have seen some very fine theatrical storms in my time; they did these things very well in the days of the elder Irving at the Lyceum, but I never enjoyed any of those tempests half so much as a storm I once watched from the wings, while Sir Frank Benson was playing King Lear. Everything, of course, was pitchy dark, save where a farthing light was glimmering in some odd corner. By this light crouched a squat form, that of the assistant stage-manager. In one hand he held the Prompt Copy of the Play, with all the cues duly indicated in it. He held it up as close as he could to the miserable glimmer, and had evidently as much as he could do to see the script with its various interlineetions and noughts and crosses, and all sorts of queer hieroglyphics which mean a great deal to a stage-manager's eye. But in the other hand he held a drumstick, and coming nearer I saw that the big drum was beside him on the boards, and that near at hand dim figures stood ready for some mysterious service. A voice is heard from somewhere:

"Blow, winds, and crack your cheeks! Rage! Blow
   You cataracts and hurricanes, spout
Till you have drench'd your steeples, drown'd the cocks,
You sulphurous and thought-executing fires,
Vaunt-couriers to oak-cleaving thunderbolts,
Singe my white head; and then, all-shaking thunder—"

And so on. And all the while the man with the big drum was commenting on the text. At certain points, bang! would come the drumstick on the drum, and that gave the cue to the man who stood by the thunder-sheet, which he caused to waggle violently, and at the same moment "Props" released his lightnings. It was far better behind than in front, to my taste, at all events. And so a man of letters of very great distinction once said to me:

"I've been reading your 'Great God Pan.' I didn't make much of it. Confused, it seemed to me. But when I read the Introduction, I said to myself: 'Good heavens! Here's a man who writes as well as I do!'"

And I may say that the literary gentleman meant this as a very great compliment; indeed so it was.

Well, we have been speaking a little of the stage. And in the earlier rehearsals of a play a good deal is taken for granted, or indicated by the gentleman in charge. I am speaking of the old days, be it understood, and of the Shakespearean Touring Company in the provinces. The company is assembling in the wings in small groups, one strolling in after another, some of them with the cheerful look of those who have partaken of refreshment. On the whole the men keep together, and the women talk to each other. The curtain is down, and by it is a deal table and a couple of windsor chairs—or it may be a couple of golden thrones. At the table sit the stage-manager and his assistant, occupied with the prompt copies and various documents connected with the business of the morning. Above their heads burns the T-piece; piping in the shape of a capital T, with the top bar pierced and flaming with gas-jets. The stage-manager looks at his watch. "Five past eleven! All ready for the Procession! March off."

The stage-manager has risen from his windsor chair—or throne, as the case may be—and is looking up stage with his back to the curtain. As he says, "March off," he indicates the music that isn't there:

"Too-too, too-too—too-too, tootery-too, too-too," in something like the time and tune of the music as it will be "on the night"; stamping with one foot on the stage to increase the realism of the performance. The old stage direction reads something like: "A sennet within. Culverins shot off," and accordingly the stage-manager interrupts his "too-tooing" at intervals:

"Too-too, tootery-too! Bang!" bringing his practicable foot down on the boards with a terrific crash.

"Too-too-too, too-too: Bang!"

Then: "March over. Flourish of Trumpets. Tara-tara-tara, ta-ta-ta. Curtain up! Tara-tara, ta-ta-ta-ta-tara. Procession on."

## Things Near and Far

The Procession of Knights and Ladies which has been forming in the dusty obscurity of the wings begins to advance and cross an imaginary line which marks the place where the scenery will be on the night. They make more especially for a position up stage (L.U.E.) where there will be, at the proper time, a Gothic archway. The " taras " are still going on. They are violently interrupted.

" Where's the Rush-strewer ? " howls the stage-manager. " Mr. Machen ! (fff) Mr. Machen ! Lobbit ! (to the hovering call-boy) Call Mr. Machen ! (To the Procession) Go back. I am going to have this done properly, if we have to stay all day for it."

The call-boy rushes violently into the darkness. His voice is heard vociferating " Mr. Machen ! " in passages and on stairs. Finally, Mr. Machen appears, looking flurried or sulky, as the case may be. The stage-manager, who had been discussing beer with Mr. Machen a short quarter of an hour before, in a friendly and familiar manner, is now, very properly, distant and official.

" Mr. Machen, I wish you would contrive to be more punctual. Better be an hour too soon on the stage than a second too late. You can't learn to act, you know, by staying away from rehearsal ! "

Mr. Machen murmurs something about " ten minutes allowed for variation of clocks." The stage-manager grunts impatiently. Mr. Machen places himself at the head of the procession with an imaginary bundle of rushes on his left arm. The too-tooing, the banging, the tara-ing are done all over again, and at last the stage-manager announces: " Flourish over "—and the play begins.

In other words, after the little difficulties and delays that I have indicated, " The Three Impostors " was published in the Keynotes Series at the Bodley Head. It didn't do so well as " The Great God Pan." The title was a bad one. Then, as my French colleague, the late P. J. Toulet, said to me afterwards: " *Ce livre est trop fumiste, ou pas assez fumiste* "; the farce and the tragedy in it were not well mixed. And again, there had been some ugly scandals in the summer of '95, which had made people impatient with reading matter that was not obviously and obtrusively " healthy "; and so, for one reason or another, " The Three Impostors " failed to set the Fleet Ditch on fire.

Whereupon I began to think about my next book. I had done, as I have said, with Stevensonianism and White Powders; now we were to have something entirely new. " Tara, tara, tara ! "—in the stage-manager's manner. This time there was to be no doubt of it. " Everybody ready for the Great Romance ! "

I started fair. There was to be something different from the former books: I knew that. But I hadn't the remotest notion of what this new book was to be about. I used to go out in the morning and pace the more deserted Bloomsbury squares and wonder very much what it would be like. I got the hint I wanted at last from a most interesting essay by Mr. Charles Whibley, written by way of Introduction to " Tristram Shandy." Mr. Whibley was discussing the picaresque in literature. He pointed out that while "Gil Blas" and its early Spanish originals represented the picaresque of the body, and "Don Quixote" was picaresque both of mind and body, "Tristram Shandy" was picaresque of the mind alone. The wandering in that extraordinary book is, in other words, noumenal, not phenomenal. I caught hold of that notion: the thought that a literary idea may be presented from the mental as well as the physical side of things, and said to myself: "I will write a 'Robinson Crusoe' of the mind." That was the beginning of "The Hill of Dreams." It was to represent loneliness not of body on a desert island, but loneliness of soul and mind and spirit in the midst of myriads and myriads of men. I had some practical experience of this state to help me; not altogether in vain had I been constrained to dwell in Clarendon Road and to have my habitation in the tents of Notting Hill Gate. I immediately marked down all these old experiences as a valuable asset in the undertaking of my task: I knew what it was to live on a little in a little room, what it meant to wander day after day, week after week, month after month through the *inextricabilis error* of the London streets, to tread a grey labyrinth whose paths had no issue, no escape, no end. I had known as a mere lad how terrible it was on a gloomy winter's evening to go out because the little room had become intolerable, to go out walking through those multitudinous streets stretching to beyond and beyond, to see the light of kindly fires leaping on the walls, to see friendly faces welcoming father or husband or brother, to hear laughter or a song sounding from within, perhaps to catch a half glimpse of the faces of the lovers as they looked out, happy, into the dark night. All this had been my daily practice and use for a long while; I was qualified then, in a measure, to describe the fate of a Robinson Crusoe cast on the desert island of the tremendous and terrible London. Thus was accomplished what Garrick called, much to the Doctor's amusement, the " first concoction " of the book.

I am sorry that I cannot trace the further steps in its elaboration with a like minuteness. All this time I was getting my green-mounted review cuttings of " The Three Impostors." I have kept them, I know, for I keep all my reviews, but I cannot lay my hands on them. I believe, though, that their general import was that I was something of a pretentious ass and that my horrors were all humbug; and for some obscure reason, which I cannot undertake to explain, these notices cheered me on immensely in my new work.

" I cannot undertake to explain "; that is the very truth. Why should a man whose only life consists in writing books feel highly elated at being told on good authority that he is utterly and entirely incapable of doing anything of the kind; that he is clever, perhaps, in a thin sort of way, but that his most prized effects at which he has evidently toiled—as the reviewer declares—with most laborious pains miss fire completely; that his endeavours to be this, that and the other are really pathetic in their utter failure; that his lightnings and thunderings are effects of the property man? I do not know why this should be so, and perhaps if I knew I should not tell; but I think I know that there are deep things in psychology, in the real psychology, not in the muck-heap of the psycho-analytical chemists. At all events, I know that when I read a review which ended, say, with: " We can only wish Mr. Machen better luck with his next bag of thaumaturgic tricks," I would be much uplifted, and go out and pace Mecklenburgh Square and the old graveyard by Heathcote Street in a happy mood of invention, feeling that the new book lay all simple and plain before me.

So, thus cheered and highly comforted, I went on my daily tours about the Bloomsbury squares, about waste places abutting on the King's Cross Road, about the wonderlands of Barnsbury, taking with me the problem of this great book that was to be made; this book that was to be the better part of me. Why, it was only the other day that a friend, who is curious like myself, in the remaining oddities of London, took me for a short stroll near the Gray's Inn Road.

" I think," said he, " that I can show you something that you will like."

In his voice was the pride of the collector, who takes his keys, opens his safe, and draws out the rich case, containing " Pickwick " in the original numbers, with the cancelled plates, unopened leaves, all the advertisements preserved, perfect condition, autograph letter signed " Charles Dickens," giving the source of the character of Sam Weller in separate portfolio: all the pride of one who possesses such a treasure was in the voice of my friend.

*Things Near and Far*

He led me round corner after corner, by turns and ways that became more and more obscure. Then, elated, he said : " There ! "

In the by-street I saw a queer house, standing in a sunken yard away from the pavement. It was painted in cream colour, and grotesque heads, intended to be mediæval, were peppered over its frontage. I knew it well.

" I never expected to see that again," I said. " I thought it would have been pulled down long ago ; like the ' Rows ' that once led from Great Coram Street. And, unless I am mistaken, we shall find Hebrew letters inscribed on plaster shields applied to the house front."

The Hebrew inscriptions were still there ; very faint, but still there. I had last seen them in '95–'96 when I was entangled in the most intricate problems of " The Hill of Dreams."

I have told already some of the troubles of the book : the battle of the second chapter, the notion sought in vain for three weeks : the affair of the fifth chapter when I lost my way completely and wrote many thousands of words that had to be rejected. Nearly all the journey, from the autumn of 1895 to the spring of 1897, there were doubts and trials and questionings : after all, was it not hopeless ; would it not be better to tear it up and start afresh on a new book ? In the summer of 1896, when I was in the thick of these perplexities, I spent a month in Provence and Languedoc, visiting places the very names of which are incantations : Arles, Avignon, Nîmes, Montpellier, Beaucaire, famed Tarascon by Rhone ; and I saw how the sun can shine on the white cliff road by Marsilho—to give the city its Provençal name, which you must pronounce, as near as may be, Mar-see-yo-ho. And the changing of the colours of the sea there, as the sun sank and brief twilight gathered and the moon rose: here were marvels and beauties that sank deeply into the heart.

A wonderful land, indeed. The olive garths, of such a silvery, dim green as our northern seas sometimes put on near the land, the scented rosemary growing as a weed by the roadside, the walls of Avignon seen by sunset light, the great Roman arenas, still in use for bull-fights, a matter not remote from their original purpose, the Temple of Diana at Nîmes, no ruin, but a perfect building into which the priest of Diana might well enter as you viewed the portal from the modern street; and above all the splendour of that southern sun shining on white rocks, on the dark cypresses, on the white arch which looked as clear and fine as if it had been built a year, which was eighteen hundred years old or more: all these are Provence; not at all forgetting the Bouillabaisse which Pascal makes in the Old Port, Pascal who roasts his incomparable partridges before a fire of vine boughs. More than once I felt that I had made a journey rather in time than space, that these black cypresses and clear white walls and green and silvery olives were present not in our day but in the old Roman world.

The last few days of my visit to Provence I spent in a little hotel at a place called Roucas Blanc, not far from Marseilles. The hotel, sheltered by the white rock and the dark green woods, had been built on the very verge of the sea, and in the morning I would open the door-window of my apartment and stand on a platform, but a few feet above the water. I would lean over the low wall, and wonder at the jewelled glory of the Mediterranean blue beneath the mounting sun—and my heart was at home, in Gray's Inn, in my old Japanese bureau, in the litter of papers that awaited me there, in the wretched book that I was struggling to make. *Aqui esta encerrado el alma del licenciado.* What have I said of the paradox of life, that its actualities are so nauseous that men will do anything to escape from them? And here was I, free to enjoy the sun on the Provençal sea and the wonder of the Roman world, hankering after the world of anguish and difficulty and disappointment that I had made for myself in grim Verulam Buildings, amidst the London fogs.

And so I got back and found that the labour of months had been wasted, and set to work to break and remake. The book was finished, somehow, in the March of 1897, and just then, as if he had come upon his cue, a new publisher, Mr. Grant Richards, wrote to me asking if I had any manuscripts that I should like to have published. I saw him and left " The Hill of Dreams " with him. He did not take long to make up his mind about it. He would have none of it, and he wrote advising me by no means to publish the book; for, he said, it would do me no credit. What he meant was that it was not in the least like " The Three Impostors," and it took him ten years before he saw light on the subject, for it was the firm of Grant Richards that published " The Hill of Dreams " in 1907.

Some amusing reviews appeared. The "Daily Graphic" said, very truly, that the book was not of much practical interest, and the "Outlook" confirmed this dictum by stating that there was "scarcely a place for it in the widest utilitarian view." "Will readily impress a reader of quiet tastes," declared the gentler "Scotsman." "Nothing that more quickly tends to tedium," corrected the "Manchester Guardian": naturally enough, if the "Athenæum" was right in saying that "the main matter of regret is the utter formlessness and the arid inhumanity of his work." "Well written, but written not quite well enough," was the fatal sentence of the "Chronicle." And so on, and so on. I will not disguise the fact that some of the notices were very good indeed; but it has always been the other sort of review that has heartened me, and so forthwith I set about writing a book in high spirits. This turned out to be "The Secret Glory," which was published in the spring of 1922. This book also was on the whole very well reviewed, though it is as queer as queer can be—I am afraid I must say that the bridge is not nearly so well kept now as in the brave days of old. But one reviewer stood out boldly, and him I will quote in full, and so make an end of talking about reviews, which some authors jeer at, which I treasure with reverent care.

"Even if we wished, we could not tell the story of 'The Secret Glory.' Mr. Machen manages to combine an onslaught on the publicschool system with some watery Paterian mysticism. Personally, we have an equal dislike of those who belaud and those who denigrate the public-school system. Besides, 'there ain't no sich person'; there are as many systems as there are public schools. But Ambrose Meyrick, if he could have been jerked for a moment by his creator into a semblance of real existence, would justify the worst outrages wrought upon him by his equally incredible *alma mater*. He is a sentimental philanderer with æsthetic Catholicism, a mystical Celtic dreamer, a Soho Bohemian (before Soho was ruined, of course); but these crimes are as nothing compared to his incorrigible penchant for 'poetic prose.' Mr. Machen has encouraged him in it. He will have a great deal more to answer for in the day of judgment than the schoolmaster who tried to beat him out of it."

There! That notice, which appeared in "The Nation and the Athenæum," was signed by Mr. J. Middleton Murry, generally recognised as being one of the most eminent literary critics of the day, if he is not rather to be accounted as the most eminent literary critic of the day. He is also, as a fellow-writer assured me, regarded as "the leader of the younger intelligentsia." Anyhow, I like a man who speaks his mind. I try to do so myself, sometimes.

And "there!" again. I think I have written enough about the manner in which I thought of my books, the manner in which I wrote my books, the manner in which I broke down more or less lamentably in the beginning, the middle and the end of my books, the manner in which they were welcomed by eager publishers, and the manner in which they finally tottered into print and were acclaimed by the Press. Enough has been said on all these topics, and perhaps a good deal too much for the patience of a weary world.

Let us now be brief on this matter. The year 1898 I spent in the service of " Literature," a weekly journal that had just been started by " The Times." In 1899 I wrote " Hieroglyphics " and " The White People," and the first chapter of " A Fragment of Life." Then a great sorrow which had long been threatened fell upon me: I was once more alone.

## Chapter IX

IT was somewhere about the autumn of 1899 that I began to be conscious that the world was being presented to me at a new angle. I find now an extreme difficulty in the choice of words to convey my meaning; "a new angle" is clumsy enough, " here in this world he changed his life" is far too high in its associations; but there certainly came to be a strangeness in the proportion of things, both in things exterior and interior. And it is in these latter that I held and still hold that the true wonder, the true mystery, the true miracle reside. There is the old proverb, of course: "Seeing is believing" and, for once, the old proverb is widely astray. All phenomenal perception is apt to be deceitful, and very often is deceitful. This is in the nature of things, as Berkeley pointed out a very long time ago. That castle tower that looks round in the distance is found to be square when you get a little nearer to it; the red and golden glory and the magic architecture of the sunset cloud would change, if you were in it, into something like a London fog. And if it be objected: "Yes, exactly; when you are far away from an object you see it incorrectly, but when you come near it you see it correctly"—that is not so. If you were near enough to the tower, with your nose within six inches of it, you only see a certain limited extent of stone surface; the tower, *qua* tower, has entirely disappeared. But you see the stone surface accurately? No, you don't. The ant crawling up it has a wildly different vision and perception of that stone surface from your vision and perception; and a microscope gives yet another vision, different from either; and as magnification must be infinite in potentiality, though not *in actu*, it is quite clear that no one can ever see the truth of any external object presented to the eyes: there must always be, in theory and perhaps, eventually, in fact, another microscope of still higher magnifying power, which will entirely change the aspect of the thing seen. And thus, without tedious specification and example of all the other senses, I mustn't even call the poker stiff, lest the man in the chair on the other side of the fire take it up and tie it into a knot before my eyes, proving that I have been talking foolishly. And get the rarest Bordeaux that money can buy, and offer Bill the navvy a glass; and watch his face as he calls for ale to wash that muck, that . . . something muck, out of his mouth.

All this, of course, is mere philosophic A B C, and if I thought this book likely to penetrate into philosophic circles I should apologise for a clumsy rehash of Berkeley's irresistible conclusions; but I do not think that the readers of "Mind" will trouble themselves about me; and I am afraid that those of us who have not been rectified by the study of philosophy are still inclined to think that seeing is believing and that some things are hard and others soft, and so on. And, no doubt, there is a kind of relative and highly inferior sort of truth in these propositions: don't knock your head against a stone wall, for instance, is a perfectly sound bit of practical advice, since, considered in relation to your skull, the stone wall *is* hard and will hurt. And so with " seeing is believing " : in nine hundred and ninety-nine cases out of a thousand you will be absolutely correct in saying : " Hullo ! There's old Secretan walking up the garden path." But there is that thousandth—or millionth—case in which it turns out that old Secretan was busy in Tibet or busy dying at the moment you were quite certain that you saw him approaching the hall-door of The Cedars : and then where is your " seeing is believing " maxim ? I had a curious instance of this in the midst of the famous " Angels of Mons " controversy. An officer of very high distinction wrote to me from the front, and described a most remarkable experience which had been vouchsafed to him and to others during the retreat of August, 1914. The battle of Le Cateau was fought on August 26th. My correspondent's division, as he writes—his letter is quoted at length in the Introduction to the second edition of " The Bowmen " —was heavily shelled, " had a bad time of it," but retired in good order. It was on the march all the night of the 26th, and throughout August 27th, with only about two hours' rest.

" By the night of the 27th we were all absolutely worn out with fatigue—both bodily and mental fatigue. No doubt we also suffered to a certain extent from shock ; but the retirement still continued in excellent order, and I feel sure that our mental faculties were still quite sound and in good working condition. On the night of the 27th I was riding along in the column with two other officers. We had been talking and doing our best to keep from falling asleep on our horses. As we rode along I became conscious of the fact that, in the fields on both sides of the road along which we were marching, I could see a very large body of horsemen. These horsemen had the appearance of squadrons of cavalry, and they seemed to be riding across the fields and going in the same direction as we were going, and keeping level with us. The night was not very dark, and I fancied that I could see squadron upon squadron of these cavalrymen quite distinctly. I did not say a word about it at first, but I watched them for about twenty minutes. The other two officers had stopped talking. At last one of them asked me if I saw anything in the fields. I then told him what I had seen. The third officer then confessed that he too had been watching these horsemen for the past twenty minutes. So convinced were we that they were really cavalry that, at the next halt, one of the officers took a party of men out to reconnoitre, and found no one there. . . . The same phenomenon was seen by many men in our column. . . . I myself am absolutely convinced that I saw these horsemen; and I feel sure that they did not exist only in my imagination."

Now I have not the faintest notion what really happened to the Colonel, to the two officers and to many of the men in the column. What concerns us for the moment is that these people were at first perfectly certain that they saw sensible objects, that is, cavalrymen, and then were perfectly certain that there were no sensible objects to see; and therefore it may be concluded from this instance and from many instances, of like sort, that the senses are deceptive; that the world of the senses is very largely a world of illusion and delusion. To give a sharp example of what I mean: I would say that the old story of the oak and the dryad is much nearer to the real and final truth about the oak than the scientific classification and description of the tree in a manual of Dendrology. Not that I believe that a spirit in the shape of a beautiful woman of another order of being to our own is somehow bound up with the life of the oak tree; but I do believe that the truth about the oak tree—as about all else—is a great mystery, which is quite beyond the purview of all sensible—that is scientific—perception and enquiry.

And so, when I speak of that singular rearrangement of the world into which I entered in the late summer of 1899, I do not desire to lay much stress on the sensible, or material, phenomena which were presented to me. I marvel, but I marvel with caution, remembering the manifold deceits of the senses, the phantasmagoria or shadow show that they are always displaying before us; remembering also that when the super-normal is manifested it is usually, in nine cases out of ten, irrelevant and insignificant. For example, in the case of old Secretan, seen walking up the path to the hall-door of The Cedars, but discovered afterwards to have an undoubted *alibi*, either on his dying bed or in Tibet. Suppose the latter case, suppose that Secretan returns and that you collar him and ask him if he remembers what he was doing about five o'clock of the afternoon of June 28th.

"What makes you ask that?" he may reply, likely enough. "I thought it rum at the time. Here's the entry in my diary. 'June 28th. Had rank goat and tea with rancid butter in it in the afternoon. Thought of the jolly tea and tennis parties at The Cedars and wondered how old Jones was getting on in the City.'"

And, it seems shocking, but it is probably the truth, that if Secretan had been really engaged, not in Tibet but in dying, his thought, the force which projected his shadow on that gravel path of The Cedars, Thames Ditton, was: "Beastly taste in my mouth! Wish I could get round to old Jones's and wash it out with a glass of his pre-war whiskey. Eh?" . . . and the silence.

And all this, as I say, is irrelevant and insignificant; and then again the rats and snakes and other objects seen by the delirium tremens patient; they really don't matter—save to the patient aforesaid, who, of course, is quite sure that they are there. So, again, I distrust the senses, and though I wondered and still wonder, I make nothing much of the great gusts of incense that were blown in those days into my nostrils, of the odours of rare gums that seemed to fume before invisible altars in Holborn, in Claremont Square, in grey streets of Clerkenwell, of the savours of the sanctuary that were perceived by me in all manner of grim London wastes and wanderings. One would like to think of the Knights of the Grail who were ware of the "odour of all the rarest spiceries in the world " before the Vision was given to them: but . . . if one is not a Knight of the Grail, but far otherwise?

Then, again, there was that morning, a bright, keen morning of November it seems in my recollection, when I was walking up Rosebery Avenue with a friend, and suddenly became aware of a strange sensation, and as suddenly recollected the old proverb: "walking on air." I remember thinking at the time: "this is incredible"; and yet it was a fact. The pavement of that horrible street had suddenly become, not air, certainly, but resilient; the impact of my feet upon it was buoyant; the sensation was delicious. I may mention that that very morning I had made a certain interior resolution; but I do not venture for one moment to connect this with that; I only tell what happened to me. I make no deductions, nor do I venture to conclude anything: remembering always that neither seeing nor smelling nor feeling is necessarily believing. But so it was, exactly as I have told it.

And then there was one afternoon in my sitting-room at 4 Verulam Buildings, Gray's Inn. I was sitting in my chair, and the wall trembled and the pictures on the wall shook and shivered before my eyes, as if a sudden wind had blown into the room. Let me hasten to say that there was no wind, no actual wind, that is; and that I knew at the time that there was no wind, and was, in consequence, not a little alarmed, not knowing what would happen next. And I must already correct my phrase: I have said that the pictures on the wall opposite to the window that looked on the garden of the Inn "shook and shivered." It is not quite just: trembled, dilated, became misty in their outlines; seemed on the point of disappearing altogether, and then shuddered and contracted back again into their proper form and solidity: that is the closest description of what I witnessed: with a shaking heart, and with a sense that something, I knew not what, was also being shaken to its foundations. This is all wonderful? I suppose that it is; but let me here say firmly that I consider an act of kindness to a wretched mangy kitten to be much more important.

But now comes a puzzle. We are highly composite beings. We all know that a stomach-ache may make a man very miserable, and I believe that science is beginning to admit that misery may give a man a very bad stomach-ache. There are old phrases about a "sinking heart," and a man's heart being "in his boots." Well, it seems that the heart does not sink, but that the stomach does, when subjected to certain emotional perturbations. Only this morning I was reading in the paper of new radiographic experiments which showed that under certain stimulations of horror or fear or grief the stomach sometimes falls from one to three inches, and the doctor who was conducting the experiments declared that there was the brighter side; that he had mentioned possible "pints of bitter" to some of his subjects, with the result that there was a perceptible and upward movement of the organ in question. And so the play goes round in a ring, with a constant action and reaction of the physical and mental—or psychical, or spiritual—and it will often be difficult to say where the prime cause resides: in the stomach, in the brain, or in the immortal spirit. I have already professed my belief that the true wonder, the true miracle are of the spirit, not of the body; I here confess that in certain cases I find it difficult to disentangle the two worlds of our apprehension, that is to say definitely that the sensible thing, the phenomenal thing, is always and invariably without any true significance.

And so with that afternoon's work in Gray's Inn. The shivering pictures that seemed on the point to dissolve and return into chaos, the sensible thrill of delight that accompanied this strange manifestation—I had forgotten that part of the experience—such phenomena as these may be producible, for all I know, by drugs. You can, at all events, see far more wonderful things than anything that I saw by taking a sufficient dose of Anhelonium Lewinii and then shutting your eyes. But . . .

I had better begin at the beginning. That afternoon I was in a state of very dreadful misery and desolation and dereliction of soul. It is strange, but the most dreadful pangs of grief are generally, I think, bearable in the moment of their impact. With the wounds of the spirit, it is as with the wounds of the body; a certain anæsthesia accompanies the actual fall of the blow. I once fell backwards from some little height, and my skull lighting on the edge of a brick, I remained unconscious for more than half an hour. And I remember distinctly that the sensation at the very moment of the crash was that of being lifted and gently laid on the softest of all downy pillows; it was only when I raised myself slowly, not in the least aware that I had been unconscious, that I felt the pain of the great bleeding wound at the back of my head, and a dismal, heavy throbbing of the brow. So with the wounds of the soul; I had borne what had to be borne with some measure of solidity and stolidity; the torture of six years of lamentable expectation had, as I supposed, seared and burned my spirit into dull, insensitive acquiescence: but I was mistaken. A horror of soul that cannot be uttered descended upon me, on that dim, far-off afternoon in Gray's Inn; I was beside myself with dismay and torment; I could not endure my own being. And then a process suggested itself to me, as having the possibility of relief, and without crediting what I had heard of this process or indeed having any precise knowledge of it or of its results, I did what had to be done—I hasten to add without any more exalted motives than those which urge a man with a raging toothache to get laudanum and take it with all convenient speed. I suffered from a more raging pain than that of any toothache, and I wanted that pain to be dulled; that was all.

Well, I made my experiment, expecting, very doubtfully, almost incredulously, certain results. The results that I obtained were totally different from my expectations. I couldn't have hypnotised, or " magnetised," or mesmerised, or suggested, or Coué'd, or in any way bedevilled myself into the obtained condition for the good reason that I had never heard of it, had no faintest notion of it, and was, in fact, as I have stated, not a little alarmed by it, half-thinking, if the truth be told, that I was very near to death. I may state, by the way, that in the course of a pretty extensive acquaintance with "occult" company, I only once heard of anything at all comparable with this strange adventure of mine. A man was running on, foolishly and uncritically enough, about his various occult experiences—they were of little interest as a whole—and talked at last of some sojourn that he had made amongst the Moors of Northern Africa. Here, he said, he had met a man who had known wonders, and he proceeded to tell them. There was nothing very wonderful, so far as I can remember; but the Moor or Arab of the story had an experience like enough to mine—I need not say that I had not mentioned it nor so much as hinted it to my occult acquaintance. The African also had seen the walls shiver and prepare for dissolution, had felt that the world was shaken, and that his heart was shaken within him. Mr. Jones-Robinson told the tale without any sense, apparently, that it had any special significance; it was part of his occult pack, that was all; and he went on to some sick rubbish about the "correspondence" of the Tarot Trumps with the letters of the Hebrew Alphabet; and this nonsense he discussed with real relish and a high sense of its infinite importance. I think that he alone knew the real "attribution" of the aforesaid Tarot Trumps, but he "had received it under pledge and was not at liberty to speak"—for which inhibition I was deeply thankful, having little patience for solemn hanky-panky or Abracadabras of any sort. But in ending his story of the

Enchanted Moor, he said that this man, who had seen the material world quivering and fading before his eyes, had received, in some manner not indicated, a command or an intimation that he must " leave everything " ; and this he could not do, having a wife and children. And I must say at once that being pretty well acquainted with Jones-Robinson and all his type, I should have paid no more attention to his story of the Moor than I paid to his story of the Tarot Trumps—if it had not been for something which I knew and kept to myself. As it was, I heard the tale and the injunction, and wondered deeply, and still wonder.

But now to our point : the connection between material or sensible things and spiritual things, the question whether the former are ever of any real consequence or significance. As I have said before, the evidence that Home the medium rose " miraculously "—to adopt a convenient shorthand—into the air seems to me good ; but is such a phenomenon of any more true consequence than the phenomenon of Hydrogen gas rising into the air from the admixture of water, zinc and sulphuric acid ? And so, were the incense clouds that came to my nostrils in places where, assuredly, no material incense smoked, of consequence ? Was the billowy and resilient pavement of detestable Rosebery Avenue of consequence ? Were the pictures that shivered and wavered on the unstable wall of consequence ? I do not know ; but I am sure that the state which followed this last experience was of high consequence. For when I rose, afraid, and broke off the process in which I had been engaged, I found to my

## Things Near and Far

utter amazement that everything within had been changed. Amazement; for the utmost that I had hoped from my experiment was a temporary dulling of the consciousness, a brief opium oblivion of my troubles. And what I received was not mere dull lack of painful sensation, but a peace of the spirit that was quite ineffable, a knowledge that all hurts and doles and wounds were healed, that that which was broken was reunited. Everything, of body and of mind, was resolved into an infinite and an exquisite delight; into a joy so great that—let this be duly noted—it became almost intolerable in its ecstasy. I remember thinking at the time: " There is wine so strong that no earthly vessels can hold it ": joy threatened to become an agony, that must shatter all. Emily Brontë, describing the state of Heathcliff soon before his death, has described just such a condition; I have often wondered how she knew of it.

But this was later. For that day and for many days afterwards I was dissolved in bliss, into a sort of rapture of life which has no parallel that I can think of, which has, therefore, no analogies by which it may be made more plain. The vine and the exultation of the vine are solemn and ancient and approved figures of the joys of the interior life, but these are not quite to my purpose. I can only fall back on little things, and quite material things. My chambers in Verulam Buildings were towards the northern portion of the Inn, and the traffic of Theobald's Road was distinct enough, distinct enough, often, to be an annoyance. But this night, the " ping, ping ! " of the omnibus bell, the grind of the many wheels upon the cobble-stones sounded to me as marvellous and tremendous chords reverberating from some mighty organ; filling the air, filling the soul and the whole being with rapture immeasurable. And another trifle, as insignificant, even more insignificant, perhaps. In the ordinary state of existence the sense of touch is exercised constantly, but almost unconsciously. Now and again it is used with intent; the buyer of old furniture acquires a sort of thumb-and-finger craft; he passes the tips of his fingers over the edges of the bureau or cabinet, and they help him to decide whether the object is an antique or a novelty. And so, I suppose, a woman choosing stuffs uses her fingers in much the same manner, learning something about the silk or velvet by the process. But in general, and very conveniently, you take up pen or pencil, or place your hand on the back of the chair without any distinct consciousness of the impact of your flesh on these exterior objects: unless, that is, your hand encounter some unexpected object which insists on notice, such as a pin point or a rusty nail. But in these strange days of which I am speaking touch became an exquisite and conscious pleasure; I could not so much as place my hand on the table before me without experiencing a thrill of delight which was not merely sensuous, but carried with it, mysteriously and wonderfully, the message of a secret and interior joy.

And one more instance. I had always been subject to headaches which visited me at intervals of five, six or seven weeks, and invariably lasted for twenty-four hours. The pain was distressing, and any movement of the head raised it into a racking, throbbing agony; I should imagine that I suffered from a kind of migraine or megrims. Late one night during the time of which I am speaking I felt the first approaches of one of these tiresome attacks. I said to myself: "I wonder whether I can stop it," and I placed the tip of the forefinger of the left hand upon my forehead. I felt the sense as of a dull shock: and the pain was gone. And though I have had my share of pains and aches since then, I have never been revisited by that particular kind of headache from that day to this.

And there was yet another matter. In a little book of mine called "The Great Return," which nobody has heard of, I have told how the Holy Grail came back for a brief while to Britain after long years. And describing some of the things that were seen and known during that happy visitation, I have written:

"The 'glow' as they call it seems more difficult to explain (than certain other matters duly related). For they say that all through the nine days, and indeed after the time had ended, there never was a man weary or sick at heart in Llantrisant, or in the country round it. For if a man felt that his work of the body or the mind was going to be too much for his strength, then there would come to him of a sudden a warm glow and a thrilling all over him and he felt as strong as a giant, and happier than he had ever been in his life before, so that lawyer and hedger each rejoiced in the task that was before him, as if it were sport and play."

Thus in the story, and thus it was with me in fact,

in that autumn and winter of 1899–1900. It was with a singular surprise that I read, in St. Adamnan, many years afterwards, how St. Columba's monks, toiling in the fields, experienced now and again the very sensation—if it be just to speak of it as a sensation—that I have described. They, too, weary with their work of reclaiming the barren land of their isle, would know that sudden glow of joy and strength and courage; and they believed that it was the prayer of their Father in God, Columba, strengthening them and inspiring them, as he knelt before the altar of the Perpetual Choir. And lest it be said that I had read Adamnan when I was a boy and had forgotten all about it consciously though I had retained it subconsciously, I must solemnly declare that this was not the case; and that when this strange experience first befell me, I was overwhelmed with astonishment, and could scarcely credit that which was actually happening. I have hesitated as to whether it should be, in strictness, called a sensation, and I still hesitate. It seems to me, and I think that I can trust my recollection, that the two worlds of sense and spirit were admirably and wonderfully mingled, so that it was difficult, or rather impossible, to distinguish the outward and sensible glow from the inward and spiritual grace. *Magnum vere sacramentum.* And all this, be it remembered, would fall out in dim Bloomsbury squares, in noisy, clattering Gray's Inn Road, in a train on the Underground, amongst hustling crowds in common streets. I mention this, not forgetful of a pretty severe rebuke which I received from a very high literary quarter on account of that little book, "The Great Return," which I have just cited. The critic noted the fact that in my book the Holy Grail was manifested to the common people, to common modern people, to Welsh tradesmen and farmers. He seemed to think this very low. It may be low, but perhaps things happen in this way sometimes; and so with me: I, by no manner of means a knight, received joys and knew wonders while the trams clanged along the Clerkenwell Road in the grey winter afternoon. So it was, and it appears to me necessary to tell the truth. As Coventry Patmore says, quoting from an earlier writer: "Let us not deny in the darkness that which we have known in the light."

And beyond all this, beyond these experiences in which things of the body and things of the spirit were mingled, there was a better world of which I saw the verges. There was no more grief; there was no more resentment, there was no more anger. The griefs that flood the heart with agony, the great sorrows of life, these were seen to be but passing trifles of no moment, like the sorrow of a little child which is past and forgotten before its tears are dry. I remember tearing up an old diary which I had kept in the bitter days of Clarendon Road, a record of struggles and starvings and desolations; I tore it up because it no longer signified anything to me. The words, I daresay, were strong enough, but the tale had become of no meaning at all. I glanced at one page and another of the tattered old notebook before I rent it, with a kind of mild curiosity as to the state of mind of the silly stranger who had written all this, and had whined so dismally.

At all events, it had nothing to do with me, and so it went into fragments and into the fire. If it could be restored to me now, I should read it all with interest and whine again and foam again *sæva indignatione;* but then I have long returned into that darkness in which, I suppose, most of our lives are spent.

There is one thing that I hope I may be spared, that is the comment of the Oriental Occult Ass. I confess that I have written all this with difficulty, and with doubt as to the decency of writing it at all, especially when the tale, if it is to be a true tale, makes it necessary for me to seem to compare, for one little moment, the saints of the company and following of St. Columba with myself. But I do hope that nobody will say: " Why, this is only Ruja-Puja! You get it all in the first chapter of the Anangasataga Raja ! It's all perfectly elementary. Little Hindu children learn their A B C out of it in the Svanka Visatvara. Why, when the Swami Vishnakanandaram Jam Ghosh was over here last summer he mentioned all these phenomena as things you have to forget before you set out on the Way. As he put it so beautifully: 'The sun arises. It gleams on the Lotus. The petals of the *bhulji* flower expand. The stars are no longer seen.' Yes, isn't he wonderful? Fancy anybody still bothering about Keats and those silly people!"

I hope, I say, that I shall be spared that. I can bear better I think the (more or less) Occidental Idiot, who will speak of Shin—the letter of the Hebrew Alphabet, not the delicate portion of our anatomy—attribute it to the Tarot Trump called the Fool, and just throw in a reference to Salt, Sulphur and Mercury.

As for me, I make no deductions, I infer nothing, I refrain from saying " therefore." Like Sancho Panza : " I come from my own vineyard ; I know nothing." Perhaps I may venture to say that I have seen a lousy, lazy tramp drinking from a roadside stream that drips cold and pure from the rock in burning weather. Then the wastrel passes on his ill way, refreshed indeed, but as lousy and lazy as ever.

*De torrente in via bibet : propterea exaltabit caput.*

## Chapter X

Mr. Charles O'Malley,
Castle O'Malley, Co. Galway.

THAT was the inscription of a card which had just been placed in my hand, as I walked along Southampton Row—on which I found myself stupidly gazing in real old Southampton Row, not the staring, blatant street that bears the name now—one fine day in the summer of 1900.

Ten minutes or so before I had been taking my morning stroll in the company of my bulldog, Juggernaut. I was accosted very politely by a stoutish, youngish, clean-shaven gentleman, well dressed, with the mere suspicion of an Irish accent.

He had said without preface of any kind:

"A fine dog you've got, sir. I should be very glad if you'd come up with me and show it to a lady I know who lives in the flats opposite."

I assented at once, feeling thoroughly in the scene, as they say on the stage. I followed him and we displayed the dog Juggernaut, certainly a noble specimen of his noble race, to the lady who, I may say at once, was a lady, and appeared to be on terms of polite acquaintance with the gentleman. Jug was admired, and the gentleman and I went down into the street again. The lady had not evinced the faintest astonishment at the introduction of a total stranger with a bulldog into her flat.

## Things Near and Far

When we were both down on the pavement of Southampton Row, the amateur of bulldogs gave me his card, and told me that I should be welcome and more than welcome if ever I found myself near Castle O'Malley, in County Galway. And so he vanished—if he ever were there, as to which I held and still hold, in a fantastic sort of way, vague doubts.

No, the flat was a perfectly quiet and unostentatious one. Nothing to drink was produced; there were no K.O. drops. The lady did not ask me to look in again some evening for a quiet game of cards with a few congenial friends. Mr. O'Malley did not say that he had salvaged a Spanish galleon wrecked beneath the rocks on which Castle O'Malley was built, and that in consequence he had more money than he knew what to do with. And I missed nothing from my pocket. That is one of the reasons why I hate rationalism, since, when it is called in, in a little difficulty or perplexity, its advices and explanations are always so stupid, so wide of the mark, so absolutely futile. Finally, from that day to this, I have never seen Mr. Charles O'Malley, of Castle O'Malley, Co. Galway, nor have I heard of him. I have forgotten to say that he did not so much as ask me my name.

I only wish that I had kept some kind of note of the very strange period which I had entered. It came about gradually, the merging of Syon into Bagdad; and I have a much dimmer recollection of the latter city. For its essence, as will be seen in the anecdote of the O'Malley, was lack of purpose, a certain fantastic confusion, a sense that something without any ratio might happen at any moment. Nothing began, nothing ended: strange people were apt to separate themselves from the crowd, to engage in queer discourse without intelligible motive or meaning, and then to sink back again, leaving no trace behind. And when events lack logical sequence or connection, it is difficult to retain them in the memory. But I believe that I do remember that on this very day of the O'Malley incident ten total strangers addressed me, without any very manifest reason and to no discernible end. We encountered in all sorts of places, in the street, in the restaurant, in the vanished Café de l'Europe in Leicester Square; the strangers uttered their mysterious messages, which to me were as incomprehensible as if they had been in cipher, and so vanished away. Indeed, looking back, I begin to wonder whether I were constantly being mistaken for someone else, who must have been exactly like me; this Someone Else being evidently a prominent member of a secret society, who would be aware of the signs and passwords of the order. For all I know, when Mr. O'Malley praised poor old Jug—he has long years ago gone to be a gargoyle on the parapet of some great Gothic church of the skies—I should have answered: " Yes, he is a fine dog, but green bulldogs with blue spots are finer." Then, it may be, the interview would have become coherent, and tending to some end, and the lady in the flat would have pressed the secret panel and have disclosed . . . I really don't know what.

That very day, I mean the day of the incident of the Bulldog, Mr. O'Malley and the Lady in the Flat, I was sitting in the Café de l'Europe with a friend, discussing various matters, when, as we rose to go a young man of a somewhat colourless and unpretending appearance, who had been sitting at the other side of the table, suddenly observed:

"I have been very much interested, sir, in your conversation, and I should very much like to hear more of it."

Again, I was in the scene. I gave him my address in Gray's Inn, and he called to see me several times, always coming at night and staying pretty late, asking me many questions about interior things. I think it was only on his last visit that I found out his odd manner of leaving the Inn, when he went away at one or half-past one in the morning. He was ignorant of the fact that the Raymond Buildings Gate and the Holborn Gate have watchers by them who will open the portals all the long night; and so when he left me he would climb the spiked wall which separates Verulam Buildings from Gray's Inn Road and make off into the gaslight. He, too, vanished, and I saw him no more.

It was some time earlier in this year that I became conscious of a very odd circumstance. It will perhaps have been noticed that I have become insensibly Stevensonian in my diction, as I have spoken of the Incident of the Bulldog, or of this or of that. That is so because the atmosphere in which I lived was becoming remarkably like the atmosphere of "The Three Impostors," which, as I have remarked, is derived from the "New Arabian" manner of R. L. Stevenson. Not only did strange and unknown and unexplained people start up from every corner, from every café table, and engage me in obscure mazes of talk, quite in the Arabian manner, but I presently became aware that something very odd indeed was happening: certain characters in "The Three Impostors" showed signs of coming to life, a feat which, perhaps, they had failed to perform before. I was once talking to a dark young man, of quiet and retiring aspect, who wore glasses —he and I had met at a place where we had to be blindfolded before we could see the light—and he told me a queer tale of the manner in which his life was in daily jeopardy. He described the doings of a fiend in human form, a man who was well known to be an expert in Black Magic, a man who hung up naked women in cupboards by hooks which pierced the flesh of their arms. This monster—I may say that there is such a person, though I can by no means go bail for the actuality of any of the misdeeds charged against him—had, for some reason which I do not recollect, taken a dislike to my dark young friend. In consequence, so I was assured, he had hired a gang in Lambeth, who were grievously to maim or preferably to slaughter the dark young man; each member of the gang receiving a retaining fee of eight shillings and sixpence a day—a sum, by the way, that sounds as if it were the face value of some mediæval coin long obsolete. I listened in wonder, for there are some absurdities so enormous that they seem to have a stunning effect on the common sense, paralysing it for the moment and inhibiting its action. It was only when I got home that it dawned upon me that I had been listening to the Young Man in Spectacles, and that he came out of "The Three Impostors."

And soon Miss Lally, another character from the book, appeared, and like her prototype discoursed most amazing tales, was the heroine of incredible adventures, would appear and disappear in a quite inexplicable manner, relating always histories before unheard of, a personage wholly diverting, enigmatic and enchanting.

And the odd thing is that it was as if these two had parts to play for a season, and played them—till the prompter's bell sounded, and the curtain fell and the lights went out. Both Miss Lally and the Young Man in Spectacles still live; but they have become useful members of society and eminently successful, as I believe, in their several employments. Thus do the King and Queen in the play go home to their flats or their lodgings after the show and enjoy cold beef, pickles and a comfortable bottle of beer.

And now I am going at last to say a good word for literature. I have said, again and again, even to tedium, that the only good that I can see in it is that it is one of the many ways of escaping from life, to be classified with Alpine Climbing, Chess, Methylated Spirit and Prussic Acid. The way I have always seen it is like this: I go out on a Sunday afternoon in March with the black north-easter blowing to take a walk up Gower Street. I say to myself: " O come ! I can't stand this," and go home and write—or try to write—a chapter in " The Hill of Dreams." Many people will say that the chapter is much worse than the street, and I daresay that they are right ; but, anyhow, it was different : it was, for me, the nearest way out of Gower Street and the black north-easter. But I believe that there may be a little more in literature than this. It is certainly the escape from life; but perhaps it is also the only means of realising and shewing life, or, at least, certain aspects of life. Here is an example to my hand. Here am I, not trying to write literature, but doing my best to tell a true tale, and I find that I can make nothing of it. I can set down the facts, or rather such of them as I remember, but I am quite conscious that I am not, in the real sense of the word, telling the truth; that is, I am not giving any sense of the very extraordinary atmosphere in which I lived in the year 1900, of the curious and indescribable impression which the events of those days made upon me; the sense that everything had altered, that everything was very strange, that I lived in daily intercourse with people who would have been impossible, unimaginable, a year before; that the figure of the world was changed utterly for me—of all this I can give no true picture, dealing as I am with what are called facts. I maintained long ago in "Hieroglyphics" that facts as facts do not signify anything or communicate anything; and I am sure that I was right, when I confess that, as a purveyor of exact information, I can make nothing of the year 1900. But, avoiding the facts, I have got a good deal nearer to the truth in the last chapter of "The Secret Glory," which describes the doings and feelings of two young people who are paying their first visit to London. *I* never bolted up to town with the house-master's parlour-maid; but truth must be told in figures.

There is one episode of this period of which I

may say a little more, that is the affair of the Secret Society. Putting two and two together, a good many years after the event, I am inclined to think that it was a mere item in the programme of strange and Arabian entertainment that was being produced for my benefit: the Secret Society was of the same order as the Incident of Mr. O'Malley and the Adventure of the Young Man who always left by the Spiked Wall, only of a more gorgeous and elaborate kind. And I must confess that it did me a great deal of good—for the time. To stand waiting at a closed door in a breathless expectation, to see it open suddenly and disclose two figures clothed in a habit that I never thought to see worn by the living, to catch for a moment the vision of a cloud of incense smoke and certain dim lights glimmering in it before the bandage was put over the eyes and the arm felt a firm grasp upon it that led the hesitating footsteps into the unknown darkness: all this was strange and admirable indeed; and strange it was to think that within a foot or two of those closely curtained windows the common life of London moved on the common pavement, as supremely unaware of what was being done within an arm's length as if our works had been the works of the other side of the moon. All this was very fine; an addition and a valuable one, as I say, to the phantasmagoria that was being presented to me. But as for anything vital in the secret order, for anything that mattered two straws to any reasonable being, there was nothing of it, and less than nothing. Among the members there were, indeed, persons of very high attainments, who, in my opinion, ought to have known better after a year's membership or less; but the society as a society was pure foolishness concerned with impotent and imbecile Abracadabras. It knew nothing whatever about anything and concealed the fact under an impressive ritual and a sonorous phraseology. It had no wisdom, even of the inferior or lower kind, in its leadership; it exercised no real scrutiny into the characters of those whom it admitted, and so it is not surprising that some of its phrases and passwords were to be read one fine morning in the papers, their setting being one of the most loathsome criminal cases of the twentieth century.

And yet it had and has an interest of a kind. It claimed, I may say, to be of very considerable antiquity, and to have been introduced into England from abroad in a singular manner. I am not quite certain as to the details, but the *mythos* imparted to members was something after this fashion. A gentleman interested in occult studies was looking round the shelves of a second-hand bookshop, where the works which attracted him were sometimes to be found. He was examining a particular volume—I forget whether its title was given—when he found between the leaves a few pages of dim manuscript, written in a character which was strange to him. The gentleman bought the book, and when he got home eagerly examined the manuscript. It was in cipher; he could make nothing of it. But on the manuscript—or, perhaps, on a separate slip laid next to it—was the address of a person in Germany. The curious investigator of secret things and hidden counsels wrote to this

*Things Near and Far*

address, obtained full particulars, the true manner of reading the cipher and, as I conjecture, a sort of commission and jurisdiction from the Unknown Heads in Germany to administer the mysteries in England. And hence arose, or re-arose, in this isle the Order of the Twilight Star. Its original foundation was assigned to the fifteenth century.

I like the story; but there was not one atom of truth in it. The Twilight Star was a stumer—or stumed—to use a very old English word. Its true date of origin was 1880–1885 at earliest. The " Cipher Manuscript " was written on paper that bore the watermark of 1809 in ink that had a faded appearance. But it contained information that could not possibly have been known to any living being in the year 1809, that was not known to any living being till twenty years later. It was, no doubt, a forgery of the early 'eighties. Its originators must have had some knowledge of Freemasonry; but, so ingeniously was this occult fraud " put upon the market " that, to the best of my belief, the flotation remains a mystery to this day. But what an entertaining mystery; and, after all, it did nobody any harm.

It must be said that the evidence of the fraudulent character of the Twilight Star does not rest merely upon the fact that the Cipher Manuscript contained a certain piece of knowledge that was not in existence in the year 1809. Any critical mind, with a tinge of occult reading, should easily have concluded that here was no ancient order from the whole nature and substance of its ritual and doctrine. For ancient rituals, whether orthodox or heterodox, are founded on one *mythos* and on one *mythos* only. They are grouped about some fact, actual or symbolic, as the ritual of Freemasonry is said to have as its centre certain events connected with the building of King Solomon's Temple, and they keep within their limits. But the Twilight Star embraced all mythologies and all mysteries of all races and all ages, and " referred " or " attributed " them to each other and proved that they all came to much the same thing; and that was enough! That was not the ancient frame of mind; it was not even the 1809 frame of mind. But it was very much the eighteen-eighty and later frame of mind.

I must say that I did not seek the Order merely in quest of odd entertainment. As I have stated in the chapter before this, I had experienced strange things—they still appear to me strange—of body, mind and spirit, and I supposed that the Order, dimly heard of, might give me some light and guidance and leading on these matters. But, as I have noted, I was mistaken; the Twilight Star shed no ray of any kind on my path.

It was towards the end of 1900 that I perceived that as I had lost sight of the admirable Syon, so Bagdad was wearing badly enough. I have seen from the train the architecture of the " White City " in these recent years. It was never anything at its best, assuredly; never anything save foolishness. Still, lit up on a summer night, with its extravagant towers and walls, pavilions and domes and minarets, with all its fretted and fantastic

## Things Near and Far

work, with its still lakes and pouring waterfalls; in those old days before the war I have no doubt that it symbolised joy and enchantment to young and simple hearts. But afterwards, when long neglect had told upon it, when winter rains had wept upon its walls and soot showers had drifted on its pavilions, when the summer suns had scorched its whiteness, and black March winds had torn its feigned embroideries and false ornaments, when many autumn storms had beat upon its plaster battlements and the waterfalls were stilled and the lakes were become obscene pits of slime and rubbish—what an ugly mockery it stood there, an idiot's city fallen into ruin, a scenic fairyland in evil days. So my Bagdad became like the " White City," magic down at heel, its enchantments silly and clumsy tricks, its mystic architecture a shabby sham, its strange encounters, meetings with people who turned out to be bores or worse than bores. You know the story of the fairy gold: at night the man who had had happy commerce with the People of the Hills found himself enriched with boundless and wonderful treasure; but in the morning the marvel of gold had all turned into a heap of dead leaves; such was my case.

And here I am moved to wonder, as I often wonder, whether what we call " fairy tales " do not in fact contain a curious wisdom and the secrets of a very strange and mysterious psychology. Take this old tale of the fairy gold and its transmutation into ugly rubbish, as an example. To most of us it is a tale and nothing more than a tale; without any reason, without any meaning, without any sort of sense or significance in it. We accept it just as a piece of picturesque fancy and nothing more; the turning of the magic gold into leaves was just a happy notion of the unknown and remote individual who made up the story. But suppose that there is something more than this: rather, something quite different from this. I am well aware, of course, of the various explanations of the fairy mythology; the fairies are the gods of the heathen come down in the world: Diana become Titania. Or the fairies are a fantasy on the small, dark people who dwelt in the land and under the land before the coming of the Celts; or they are " elementals," spirits of the four elements: there are all these accounts, and, for all I know, all may be true, each in its measure. But is it possible that there is, now and then, a more hidden and interior sense in some of the tales of the fairyland and the fairies? I am inclined to think that this may be so; that the stories may be—occasionally, not always by any means—the veils of certain rare interior experiences of mankind; experiences, I may say, which are best avoided. The gold faded into dead leaves; it may be more than an idle tale. At any rate, it was a very dismal disenchantment to me when I woke up and found that I was not the Commander of the Faithful, that the fair Circassian was, in fact, a native not of Circassia but of Clapham, that Badgad was not Bagdad at all, but a London " Exhibition " fallen into very bad repair and urgently in need of tacks and whitewash. The Palace was not habitable; rain was coming in through cracks and rents in the marble that was plaster on the head of him who for a time had been Haroun Alraschid, who now began to suspect that his real style and title was Silly Fool. And then I went on the stage, which is a world of illusion certainly, but of a much less harmful illusion than that of plaster-Bagdad and fairy gold and the hall under the hill.

I have wondered at times why there is no good novel of the stage. But a little consideration shews that there can be no such thing. George Moore wrote long ago a clever book called " A Mummer's Wife." It is a capital book, and I should think a very faithful impression of a " Cloches de Corneville " touring company in the early 'eighties. I would say of an individual " Cloches de Corneville " company, for the characters strike one as portraits of particular people; there is nothing of the universal about the book, nothing of the essence of the stage life. And it is probably impossible to write the real novel of the stage, for the good reason that the stage is not one but many. In the old days, in the days of the Crummles Company, it would have been easier. The actor of those days was supposed, till he had proved his supreme eminence in one particular line of business, to be capable of all. He was to play " Hamlet," he was also to go on in the Farce, he was to dance a hornpipe between the acts, he was always to be ready with a song; and, again, unless he were a very eminent actor indeed, he very rarely associated with people beyond the range of the call-boy's voice. The stage in those days was a world apart, and the men and women who trod it a race apart; the actor was a type, just as the sailor of Smollett's day was a type. But all that is long over; it would be very difficult to find

## Things Near and Far

a general formula to cover the life of the stage to-day. Commodore Trunnion viewed all existence as a voyage on board one of His Majesty's ships; and I knew a stage-manager who, playing skittles, avowed his determination to bring down "that O.P. skittle"; but the Commodore is dead, and the stage-manager is dying. In fact I should say that the average actor of to-day is far from being gratified when he is recognised as an actor; rather he is inclined to be ashamed of his profession. I remember that as I was talking to two stage friends on a London pavement an old man who was selling laces and studs and such matters in the gutter implored us to buy: "I was an actor once myself, gentlemen." I perceived that my friends were very far from being pleased. I think that the poor old man would have done better if he had said: "I was an officer in the Guards once myself, gentlemen." So, in brief, the actors are no longer the race apart of the old days; they mix with all sorts of people and have, naturally, become very much like all sorts of people. Some of them think that the change is for the better, others disagree. I venture no judgment save this: that they are certainly less picturesque, because less differenced than of old, and thus it is that nobody is likely to do much good with a story of the stage.

I daresay that few people outside the profession are aware that the old players had a language of their own, or rather a language which they shared with another and a widely different craft. Not merely the technical language of the stage, though that had its curiosities too. For example, I once heard George Alexander at rehearsal say to one of the company: "Too much of the old, Smith, too much of the old!" And Smith, though he had been for many years on the stage, told me afterwards that he had never heard the phrase before, and didn't know what it meant. I knew what it meant, having associated, like Mr. Lillyvick, with members of the theatrical profession in the provincial, that is more or less, the less fortunate grade. "The old" means the melodramatic style of acting, the manner which used to be associated with the name of Barry Sullivan. When an actor said, "I gave them a bit of the old," he meant that he exaggerated somewhat both in his tones and in the business of the scene; in other words, that he made it "big" and "broad."

But this is not the language I mean. Once on a provincial tour I found that the stage-manager had somehow heard of my connection with literature, and was inclined, in consequence, to suspect me a little of being, as we should say now, a "high-brow" and to resent the supposed fact. So I put him through an examination. I asked if he knew what "omees" were, in particular as to the character signified by the phrase "omee of the carser." Then as to the idioms "nunty munjare" and "nunty dinnari" and so on. He broke down badly, but he put away his evil suspicions from that moment; he knew that if I had written books in my day I had turned over a new leaf and had become a reformed character: I knew the curious speech better than he did. It is barbarous Italian, and was the lingo of old-fashioned actors and thieves.

## Chapter XI

IT is a very odd experience to go on the stage at the age of thirty-nine. It is, of course, unpractical, since at that age a man is too old to learn the business properly; but it is a great entertainment. The change was so extreme. I had always lived a very quiet life. I had few friends, few acquaintances. My life was in reading books and in writing them. All my preoccupations were literary. Every morning after breakfast I went over what I had written the night before, correcting here and there and everywhere, generally convinced that the passage which had pleased me so much as I wrote it was, after all, not magnificent. I took the bulldog for a walk from 12 to 1, and another half-hour walk in the afternoon. Then two cups of tea without milk or sugar at 4, and the rigour of the literary game till 7, and again after dinner till 11. It was a life of routine, and all its adventures, difficulties, defeats and rare triumphs were those of the written page. I did not know a single actor, and had no curiosity as to the actor's life, circumstances, customs or manners. And then, one afternoon in February, 1901, I found myself stuck up with a number of ladies and gentlemen on a thing like a greenhouse flower-pot stand, and we were all required to express suitable and varied emotions as Shylock appealed for the fulfilment of the bond which Antonio had given him. This was the first thing I had tried to do on the stage, and I believe it was the most difficult. No doubt Mr.—afterwards Sir Frank—Benson was right in saying that it was the only way to learn how to act; but gesture, facial expression, pantomime, the knack of knowing how to be individual and yet to join in effectively with the crowd; all these things are extremely difficult, very much more difficult than the art of speaking an effective line effectively.

But—very likely because the change from my former way of living was so tremendous in every respect—I found the life an enchanting one. Of course I could not have begun under happier auspices; nay, I could not have begun under any auspices half so happy. It has been said, I think, more than once, and said by men far more qualified to speak than I, that if it had not been for the Benson Company, acting as an ordered art, with its technique and tradition, would pretty well have perished out of England. The old stock companies were gone, with their manifold opportunities for learning the actor's craft. The young man who went on the stage probably walked on for six months or a year in a London production, and unless he were an exceptionally bright young fellow he learned very little. Perhaps, if he were lucky, he was promoted from a thinking part to a speaking one and uttered the line : " You don't say so ! " every night; but still he learned very little. If he became a good actor under this régime, it was a case of genius triumphing over circumstance. Of course good actors come from everywhere: from the academies, from melodramas travelling in the fit-ups, from the chorus of the musical play, from the ranks of the walkers-on in the long London run; but, as I say, these are cases of greatness overcoming difficulties. But under the training provided by the Benson Company it was a man's fault if he did not learn to act; it was pretty definite proof that there was no acting in his composition. I remember Henry Ainley saying in this very year, 1901: "Well, in the last fortnight I have played twelve different parts, and if that won't teach a man how to act, nothing will." This, I may say, was at the end of the Festival Season at Stratford-on-Avon, a strenuous and a delightful time.

But, as I say, I could have entered on the boards under no happier auspices. There was a constant succession of small parts, so graded with due tenderness both to the beginner and the audience that not much harm could be done by uneasy awkwardness, and much good was certain to be gained by the beginner. For example, I have a suspicion that the whole pack of us on that flower-pot stand in "The Merchant," all of us beginners, were about as bad as bad can be; but it really signified little. The people in front were looking at Shylock and Portia, not at us; and I don't suppose that our incapacity diminished to any calculable extent the public entertainment. Then in the next piece, "As You," I was a Forest Lord with a line. I had to say to the Banished Duke: "I'll bring you to him straight," and Oscar Asche took pains to show me that I must speak it as I moved up stage with my back to the audience; but the fortunes of the play hardly depended on that line, while I was beginning to grow a slight seed of confidence.

And how all this was an utterly different world from anything that I had ever conjectured; I cannot express the gulf that yawned between the old and the new. In the former years I struggled with words and phrases and sentences and shades of meaning implied by them : now I strove to understand how something like an attenuated pigtail could become a highly probable fifteenth-century beard and moustaches in a couple of minutes, when skilled hands were laid upon it. And I was occupied with R.U.E. and L.U.E. and 5 and 8, and how to stand so that you command the stage as F. R. B. instructed me, and the endeavour to take in and profit by the kindly tips and hints and cautions given by the elder members of the company: here was a holiday, indeed, for a man who had tried to tear the secret of literature from the thorn castle where it is concealed, who had torn his hands and his heart sadly enough in the endeavour.

I have mentioned the tips and hints of the Elder Brethren amongst the Bensonians. This was a great part of the discipline and instruction of the course. It was not only what Benson said at rehearsal, it was also what Asche or Rodney or Brydone or Swete said after the rehearsal or after the show, and often what they said was, quite rightly, highly uncomplimentary. I remember when Henry Herbert—" starring " in America now, I believe—was playing in " King John," it fell to him to pronounce the lines which speak of painting the lily and gilding refined gold. He spoke them, as I thought, with great spirit; but Brydone—dead not long ago—took him apart afterwards and talked to him for half an hour or more as to the grave mistake he had committed.

"You spoke the lines as if they were beautiful poetry," said Brydone, "and, indeed, they are. If you had been reciting them your reading would have been quite right; but not in the scene, on the stage. So-and-so—I have forgotten the name of the part—is raging against King John; he isn't thinking of the poetic beauty of the words he is using."

Now, I do not presume to judge whether Brydone were right or wrong in this criticism; such matters are too high for my small experience as an actor; but consider the enormous value to the beginner of living in such an atmosphere of thought and observation and consideration of the things of the theatre. Herbert may have come eventually to the conclusion that he had been right after all, and that Brydone was wrong; but, anyhow, he had worried the question out and weighed it in his mind, and looked at it and around it; and all that, it seems to me, is the very air in which good craftsmanship is born and nurtured and grows great and flourishes.

And so, apart from these after-confabulations and dressing-room counsels, a rehearsal in the Benson Company has always struck me as a liberal education in the player's art. Benson himself—the "Pa" of the affectionate and reverent remembrance of many hundreds of his grateful sons and scholars—has always been an imaginative poet of a high order; though somehow he has never written any poetry. Instead, he has produced Shakespeare, and perhaps he has chosen the better way. He has illuminated his text admirably, and his way was not to come down to the theatre with the whole scheme of things cut and dried in his head, with every intonation, every bit of business and every position settled immutably beforehand, but rather to approach the play, scene by scene, with a liberal and open spirit. The main conception he doubtless brought with him, but any light he could find in the process of rehearsal he would welcome heartily, no matter whether it came from one of the elder brethren or from the newest member of the company. For example, during the rehearsals of "King John" we had come to the scene wherein the Legate, Pandulph, reconciles the King to Holy Church. I was talking to the Legate at the wings during some brief interval, and ventured very tentatively to describe the symbolical embrace known as the Kiss of Peace as a possibly effective bit of business in the reconciliation scene. The Legate, interested, asked me to show him how it was done, and we went through the business. But Benson, who seemed to be considering other matters down stage, had noticed what we were about, and he called out: "I like that: we'll do it." And done it was; and I had been a little over two months in the company and on the stage!

And another instance, taken from the same play, of a Bensonian rehearsal of those days. The scene

## Things Near and Far

was the discovery of the dead body of Prince Arthur. I had to say:

"What wilt thou do, renowned Faulconbridge,
Second a villain and a murderer?"

Whereon Hubert furiously interposed:

"Lord Essex, I am none!"

And then I had to draw the cloak away from the corpse and exclaim:

"Who killed this Prince?"

And thereupon a debate arose. Should the words be spoken before the removal of the cloak? Should the cloak be removed before the uttering of the line? Should word and action be simultaneous? The point was discussed with the utmost earnestness, as a matter of vital importance, and I, feeling that I was in mighty deep waters, suggested in all humility that I should speak the words with an indicative gesture and that Hubert should step forward, appalled, and remove the cloak and discover the body of the Prince. But this started another subsidiary debate, and the rehearsal breaking off at this point, Brydone (Hubert) and Frank Rodney (Faulconbridge) were left on the Stratford stage, walking up and down, and wondering, in muttered undertones, whether it would be within the limits of possibility and stage propriety for Hubert to snatch that cloak away. Their faces were grave, earnest and perplexed. Outside in the sunshine by the Avon I encountered "Pa." He looked at me with a certain waggishness in his eye, as if he suspected bewilderment on my part, and said:

"Well, Mr. Machen, what do you think about it yourself?"

"Indeed, sir," I replied, "I don't venture to have any opinion."

And I meant what I said, for I didn't think then, and I don't think now, that it befits the entered apprentice to express his opinion, or presume to have any opinion, in the presence of past masters.

Now it may be thought that I am "guying" the Company methods in this matter of Prince Arthur's funeral cloak. I am not doing anything of the sort. I only wish I had gone on in the craft, and were now myself entitled to walk up and down the stage, debating just such a point. The matter in itself was, no doubt, small enough: a stage management in a hurry would have given a ruling and the scene would have proceeded; but under a stage-management in a hurry what would have become of the vivid interest taken in the smallest circumstance of the play by the whole company, from F. R. Benson downward?

And, by the way, I trust I am not giving the impression that the Bensonians of that day were a body of solemn pedants? I have not yet forgotten my admiration, my almost awestruck admiration, at seeing the manner in which the man who was to play King John drank home-brewed ale in a triangular parlour of the Windmill on the afternoon before the production. He drank in the manner of the ancient heroes, and he gave a very good performance at night.

## Things Near and Far

But the Stratford Festival drew to its close. On the last Saturday we were rehearsing in the morning, playing in the afternoon and playing again in the evening. Some time in the course of the day I was told that I was to play Nym in the " Merry Wives " on Monday night at Worcester. I bought the play and looked at the part and got the cuts from the Prompt Book—and I wonder why I didn't drown myself in the Avon after the show as the easiest way out of the difficulty; and if anyone wants to know why, let him read the part of Nym in " The Merry Wives of Windsor," and ask himself how he would like to learn that queer gibberish and learn how to play it in a couple of days, he having had three months' experience of the stage. But instead of drowning myself in the Avon, I . . . refreshed myself at a famous tavern of the town together with about half the company; and I think we heard the chimes at two o'clock in the morning, and it was reported that old George Weir, on being asked " to write something " in the hostess's book had written the words: " When my cue comes call me and I will answeir."

And that reminds me: At the Bensonian dinner in the year in which this great actor, George Weir, died, F. R. Benson began his speech. His manner commanded the cessation of applause, and he raised one hand, and held it high, and said:

" This year, one amongst us has answered the summons of the call-boy of the stars."

But to return to my small business. On the Sunday we travelled to Worcester, and I spent the rest of the day in a desperate struggle with Nym and "the humour of bread and cheese," and "that's the humour of it," in endeavouring to get into my memory phrases which are not merely old but old-fashioned, for Nym, like Touchstone, discourses for the most part Elizabethan catchwords which, three hundred years before, were "certain of a laugh," which the process of time and fashion has made meaningless, and phrases such as these are very difficult to learn.

But I learned them somehow or other on the Sunday, and the next morning came to the one and only rehearsal. It was not on the stage, more important things were happening there, but in the travellers' samples room of one of the Worcester inns. Of course there was no scenery, no costumes, no "props" of any kind. A few chairs indicated the set, quite sufficiently, I may say to a man of experience, but dubiously enough to a man of next to no experience. Thus, when it came to my last exit, the Assistant Stage-Manager gave his instructions somewhat as follows:

"After you have said the last words to Page, turn round and go up the flight of steps L.C., here, between these chairs. When you have got to the top, turn again and say to Page, over his shoulder: 'My name is Nym, and Falstaff loves your wife.' Then exit Left along the terrace."

Simplicity itself, to an actor, but somewhat horrifying to a beginner. And then two or three of the principals were not there—they were rehearsing other scenes, very likely, on the stage, and the Prompter's: "Mr. Rodney will come on on that cue from the right upper entrance, where that table is, and you go up to him and meet him Centre and say so and so, and then he speaks the line so and so and you cross to the Right "—with much more to the same effect. And my breath was queer and catchy, even though it was only the rehearsal, and I wondered what my voice and I would be like at night!

Well, I was paralysed with stage-fright. But I got through, somehow; and I hope the Old Woman of the Company, Miss Denvil, as admirable an actress as George Weir was an actor, meant what she said after I had made my Exit Left along the terrace. She smacked me heartily on the back, and said:

"There! I always say the nervous ones are the best!"

So the tour went on, and in the course of it I received an odd bit of promotion. I descended from the flower-pot stand in the Trial Scene of the "Merchant" and became the Clerk of the Court. I think he speaks one line and reads a letter, and that is all. It is hardly to be called a part; if the man who had to do it failed at the last moment the Business Manager or, more likely, his assistant, would be summoned and robed in the black habit and the square cap. He would be told the line and given the letter, and that would be all right. It was so small a thing that the man who "played" it was supposed not to care to do so under his own name, so I was either not in the bill at all or else I appeared as " Mr. Walter Plinge," the Mrs. Harris of the Benson Company, who often came in useful on occasions like this, or when there was a case of "doubling." There was such a person, but I believe he kept a tavern frequented by the Company.

And so I was the Clerk of the Court, and solemnly proceeded to consider within myself what a Compleat Clerk of the Court should be like. I determined, firstly, that the boy at the back of the gallery should hear what I said; but this is a general rule—and by no means the least important—which applies to all acting. My second resolution was that a really convincing Clerk would not take the faintest interest in the very emotional procedure which seems to have characterised the strict court of Venice. He would listen to all the pleadings and all the agonies with a stolid countenance. When the Doge spoke of " brassy bosoms " and " hearts of flint " and " gentle answer, Jew " and so forth, the Clerk would become stonier and stonier in his indifference, possibly reflecting inwardly that he had always thought that the appointment was a purely political one, and that now he was sure of it. " Ad captandum arguments," " Old Bailey rhetoric," " Buzfuz on the Bench," " Trying to throw dust in the eyes of the Jew," such phrases, translated, of course, into choice Venetian dialect, might be supposed to flit through the purely legal and formalistic mind of the Clerk. As for the young advocate, whose credentials the Clerk had been obliged to proclaim, well, frankly, the Clerk could not understand how the Doge, politician as he was, could permit such unprofessional rubbish as the " Quality of mercy " speech to be uttered in court at all. " Mountain pines," " wag their high tops," "twice blest," "crowned monarch better than his throne": really, really! What was the Bar coming to? The Clerk's face and attitude have become perfectly stony in their supreme indifference; he might be a thousand miles away.

But! What is that? The Bond bad in law? The plaintiff debarred from recovering, and not only that, but, *ipso facto*, liable to criminal proceedings of a highly penal character? Now, indeed, the Clerk of the Court is interested. Not that he cares twopence for Antonio or for Shylock either; but there does seem distinctly to be a flaw. The young Advocate must have a technical mind, that greatest of all blessings. The Clerk pricks up his ears, as if he were a terrier advised of the presence of a rat; he is intensely awake; he consults his authorities on the table before him; he is really inclined to think that a highly important point is at issue; he believes that the question, or something very much like it, was raised in the Dogeship of Bragadin, c. 1150. At length the Clerk of the Court is all alive.

I thought of all that, and I tried to render it as best I could. And I only mention this trivial nonsense because, to the best of my belief, it is the only instance in which I have found that doing my best and sparing no pains brought me the faintest sort of reward. As a rule, in my experience, the mere fact of taking pains has been rewarded with the malignity of scoundrels and the insults of fools.

But in this extraordinary and, as I must say, miraculous affair it was otherwise. The tour of the Benson Company drew to its close. It was now hot

## Things Near and Far

summer and we were playing a *matinée*, I think on the Whitsuntide Bank Holiday, in some theatre on the south side of the river; some theatre which in all probability is now devoted to "the pictures." It was glorious weather, there were few people in the house, and as one of the ladies of the company observed cheerfully in the wings, "People who come to see Shakespeare on an afternoon like this ought to have their noses rubbed in it." Ah, the good, gross gaiety: how few people have as this lady had, and has, the true art of it! Her remark did me a lot of good that languid, heated afternoon in the half-empty theatre; and I believe that the Clerk of the Court—we were playing the "Merchant"—was a shade wearier than usual in his utter boredom and contempt of the whole proceedings: till his moment came.

And a few days later Henry Ainley was saying to me in our dressing-room: "I am engaged by Alexander to play Paolo next year. And, do you know, Alexander said to me: 'You've got a remarkably good actor in your Company; and I couldn't even find his name in the cast. He was playing the Clerk of the Court that afternoon: he was very good indeed.'"

The great George Alexander to speak thus of the little beginner in his little shadow of a part! Well, I suppose all such taps are vanities; but there was a very happy man that night in the dressing-room, and he plied the spirit-gum and fixed on his beard for the part of the Major-Domo in the "Shrew"—two lines—with trembling, unsteady, rapturous fingers.

## Things Near and Far

A few weeks later I was engaged to play a small part in " Paolo and Francesca," but that was for the early spring of 1902, and I had to fill in. So I joined a pastoral or open-air company (almost all of whom were Bensonians), and played with them for three weeks. Then I met a friend in the Strand and said " I want a shop," and found myself rehearsing next day the part of a comic Irish servant in a sketch called " The Just Punishment "—an entirely preposterous playlet. We did a fortnight of it—two houses a night—at the Hoxton Varieties and another East-End hall, the name of which I have forgotten. At the Varieties I dressed with a very pleasant black man ; the rats ran about the dressing-rooms and passages like kittens. And the audience ! There was no question of their being all right till you began to bore them. You made your entrance as the curtain went up, and found the whole house in an uproar. Most of it was light-hearted hilarity, some of it was argument, and they argue very forcibly in Hoxton, occasionally with broken bottles. The actor's business was to drown them, and get them to listen, and amuse them—if he could—and very capital training it was. But the sketch was not booked on—and no wonder—so I went to Mr. Denton's in Maiden Lane. He sent me to Mr. Charles Terry, who was taking out a melodrama called " The Silent Vengeance," written by Mr. Harry Grattan round the personality of Mr. Silward, that wonderful animal impersonator. From first to last I played three parts in " The Silent Vengeance "—a solicitor, a doctor and a barber—and it only ran six weeks. But for the last

*Things Near and Far*

week of the run I had been rehearsing the part of an old actor in the farcical comedy of "The Varsity Belle." Then at the end of a fortnight, for one reason or another, I had to change this rôle for that of a University Don; and there were over two hundred cues in the first act, and I had only a week for study! The manager was an entirely honest but boorish fellow, and I gave him my notice; "bunged in my notice" would be more idiomatic. The day I left "The Varsity Belle" company I got an engagement from an old Bensonian friend to play for a fortnight or so in Old Comedy down in the western country, and a delightful engagement it turned out. We all knew each other, or very soon got to know each other, and we drank beer and played skittles in tumbledown alleys behind old inns, and brewed bowls of punch, and in spite of these wild practices acted, I think, decently. Poor Ernest Cosham was the Comedian and Mr. Leon Quartermaine played the juvenile leads; and I hope he has not forgotten a famous game of Blind Hookey in a little inn at Westbury-on-Avon, the only card game that I ever enjoyed. And the morning after our last performance I went up from Andover to town and listened to Stephen Phillips reading his play, "Paolo and Francesca," to the assembled company. I had been a year on the stage, and I think I had had as varied an experience as falls to the lot of most beginners.

And here there is a great gap. There were other adventures on the stage; but enough, I think, has been said of these things. I have just told of that

*Things Near and Far*

happy moment of June, 1901, when Henry Ainley repeated to me George Alexander's kindly praise of my acting. And, indeed, that was bliss, but I believe that I received the promise of a happiness that should be deeper and more lasting one morning towards the end of August, 1921. For that morning brought a letter ending my career as a journalist.

Poor George Sampson got into grievous trouble over his innocent speculations as to so innocent a thing as an underpetticoat. I propose, therefore to say nothing about the craft of journalism, which I followed for many years.

Save only this: *Eduxit me de lacu miseriæ, et de luto fæcis. Et statuit super petram pedes meos: et direxit gressus meos.*

**THE END**

www.ingramcontent.com/pod-product-compliance
Lightning Source LLC
Chambersburg PA
CBHW020332170426
43200CB00006B/356